# HOSPICE
# DESIGN MANUAL

## For In-Patient Facilities

Timothy Moorhouse

# HOSPICE DESIGN MANUAL

## Contents

# Contents

# HOSPICE DESIGN MANUAL
## For In-Patient Facilities

Published by
Hospice Education Institute
(A Non-profit Organization)
Three Unity Square
P.O. Box 98
Machiasport, Maine 04655-0098, USA
Telephone: 207-255-8800
Website: www.hospiceworld.org

Photograph of author by Wren McMains
Book Design by Ed Ziobron

Printed in the United States of America

ISBN 0-9623438-3-8

This book breaks important new ground in the world of hospice and palliative care. As hospices and palliative care units (both in the United States and worldwide) increasingly fulfill their dreams of having a free-standing, purpose-built structure specially designed to care for their patients, there has been little literature available on in-patient hospice design.

Timothy Moorhouse's book is based on over two years of intensive research; on numerous site visits to existing hospices on two continents; on discussions and conferences with many hospice and palliative care professionals; on suggestions from hospice patients and their relatives; and on his sensitive understanding of the special needs of patients and families facing far-advanced illness. Tim is a gifted architectural designer, but he is much more than that. As exemplified by this book, his concern is for the overall well-being of hospice and palliative care patients, relatives and staff, and in providing the practical, holistic environment in which such care is best offered.

Of course, each hospice or palliative care unit will have its own vision as building plans are considered. Each community and each building site will have its own special opportunities, challenges and requirements. Each organization will need to retain highly competent local advisers from a variety of professions. But this book will reduce the need to "re-invent the wheel" as each new building is planned, because there are many basic design requirements set forth in this book which will apply to all such projects.

The Hospice Education Institute is proud to publish this book. We at the Institute thank Tim Moorhouse for his exceptional efforts towards improving end-of-life care through sound and innovative design. We also thank our many colleagues in hospice and palliative care worldwide who contributed their comments and their suggestions. We encourage you to share your experiences with us as you design and build your in-patient hospice.

Michal Galazka
Chief Executive
Hospice Education Institute

This design manual has been prepared primarily for two reasons.

Firstly, for hospice planning groups, to assist in the initial planning phase and to help in the understanding of the requirements for a hospice building and the way these function.

Secondly, for architects, to provide a research-based study of the design problems and requirements of a hospice building to assist their efforts in designing an efficient, well planned hospice building.

Several topics have been included, of which the architect will already have knowledge. Their inclusion is to supply information to laypersons on a hospice building committee.

Also because of the nature of the manual I have had to repeat information where it falls in several areas.

The research for this guide was accomplished in part by visiting almost 50 in-patient hospices around the United States and in the United Kingdom.

After touring a facility talks were held with one or more of the following: nursing staff, administrative staff, patients and their families, and the building's architect.

I would like to thank everyone who took the time out of their busy schedule to spend time talking about hospice design and function and letting me tour their facilities. All the assistance has been extremely valuable.

I would especially like to thank Michal Galazka and the Hospice Education Institute for their support with the project. Thanks also to Tom Mullinax, AIA, for his invaluable assistance.

It is my hope that hospice patients and the hospice movement will benefit from this publication.

Timothy Moorhouse BA Dipl Arch
Graduate Member Royal Institute of British Architects

February 2006

## 'Hospice'

The word "hospice" is French from the Latin *'hospitium'*, meaning **host** or **hospitality**. These are the key words in understanding the difference between traditional nursing home care and hospice care. To design a building which provides true hospice care we need to design one which offers hospitality to those who enter, a building which can allow the staff to take care of seriously ill people in an efficient manner, yet appear non-institutional and comforting to those entering as patients or as their caregivers.

**HOSPICE – a facility or program designed to provide a caring environment for supplying the physical and emotional needs of the terminally ill.**
*– Webster's Collegiate Dictionary*

**HOSPICE – a program or facility that provides palliative care and attends to the emotional, spiritual, social and financial needs of terminally ill patients at a facility or at a patient's home.**
*– The American Heritage Stedman Medical Dictionary*

An in-patient hospice facility is a building in which end-of-life care is given to seriously ill people, who often have only a short while to live.

It is a place where these people may die in a dignified manner, with as little pain and discomfort as possible.

It is a building in which those who love and care for the patients are welcomed into the facility and encouraged to spend as much time as they need with the patient, to be there with the patient as they die, and then receive continued support to help them come to terms with their bereavement.

It is a facility in which the dying person may stay involved with their care decisions to the maximum possible extent with the emphasis being on the quality not the quantity of their life.

Patients may also be admitted for symptom management, where they are under observation during a change in medication, and for respite care, where they are admitted to give some time off to their primary care givers. Both of these are usually for just a few days. Patients will often return to the hospice as they near the end of their days.

Some hospices offer residential care where a patient, though terminally ill, may live for several months, and will generally have greater mobility and independence than terminal-care patients. Some facilities are entirely devoted to residential care, whilst others have a number of rooms allocated for that purpose. Funding requirements may require a number of residential care beds to be allotted.

A full support network is required to fulfill this mission with a multidisciplinary team working together.

A hospice has to be designed as a building which can efficiently achieve all the operational requirements, be a comforting place for the patients at the end of their life and for their caregivers in their distress, and be a pleasant place for the staff and volunteers to work.

Architecture has an incredible ability to affect the moods of those who enter, and for hospice design no tools should be spared to create an environment which can give the required feelings of comfort and security.

The three principal users of a hospice are:
- Dying patients
- Distressed friends and relatives
- Medical and nursing and other staff who have to deal with dying on a daily basis

This creates a difficult design problem but with careful planning, architects can assist tremendously those in difficult times by providing a building which comforts and even delights those who use it.

## How To Use This Manual

**The manual is arranged in five sections:**

**Section 1**   General in-patient hospice design principles.

**Section 2**   Detailed notes on various aspects relative to in-patient hospice design. (Arranged alphabetically)

**Section 3**   Flowcharts detailing the way each person using a hospice progresses through a hospice building and which rooms they will use.

**Section 4**   A detailed look at each room in a hospice and its specific requirements.

**Section 5**   Two schematic designs for possible hospices, one large and one small, with a description of each one explaining the reasoning behind the designs.

**Appendix**   A list of site visits, and links to suppliers.

# HOSPICE DESIGN MANUAL

## Section 1

## Hospice team members usually include:

**Nurses** who have day-to-day contact with patients and their caregivers, and who have the primary responsibilities for coordinating the team's efforts and effective liaison between home care and in-patient nursing.

**Physicians** who must be skilled in symptom management, have the clinical skills for good hospice care, and have the interpersonal skills to work within a multidisciplinary team.

**Social Workers/Counselors** who offer special skills in caring for the social and emotional needs of dying people and their caregivers, and by supporting other members of the hospice team.

**Clergy** who can offer spiritual and religious support to patients, caregivers, and members of the hospice team.

**Physical and Occupational Therapists** whose special responsibilities to the patient are to encourage and facilitate activities and to increase independence – to help with the rehabilitation of the whole person even in the presence of advanced illness.

**Art / Music Therapists** who are playing an increasingly valuable role in encouraging the dying to seek the challenge and solace of expression through art and music.

**Complementary Therapists** who provide comfort (both physical and emotional) to patients through massage, aromatherapy, pet therapy, and other modalities.

**Pharmacists** who are critical to the team because most dying people require concurrent use of several medications.

**Administrative staff** who provide all the necessary managerial and clerical functions to allow the facility to operate and to provide the necessary enthusiasm and group leadership for it to be a success.

**Volunteers** who as full members of the hospice team offer personal and professional support to patients and caregivers, and provide any number of valuable services, from manning the reception counter to picking up an elderly relative so they may visit a patient.

**Dietitians and Nutritionists** who specialize in planning balanced diets and enhancing the tastes and textures of foods.

**Support staff** who provide the necessary services to keeping the facility running. These include: kitchen staff, maintenance staff, cleaning staff, grounds keepers, and others.

**Fund-raising staff** who are responsible in some situations for providing key funding for the program.

**Good communication between all of the team members is critical for a successful hospice.**

# HOSPICE DESIGN MANUAL

## General Design Considerations

Upon admission to a hospice, patients have generally elected to no longer receive surgical and other curative procedures and the focus is on palliative care – the relief of pain and discomfort. With the absence of surgery and invasive therapy the clinical requirements and atmosphere required in a regular medical facility can be minimized.

In order to allow the patient relief from pain and discomfort, the atmosphere in which they reside can help them along with the pain- and symptom-reducing therapies.

This includes giving the building a homelike atmosphere both with the general design – materials, building massing, etc., and the interior design – lighting, furnishings, use of color, etc. Also by providing comfortable, attractive accommodations for family members.

A balance must be achieved to provide the levels of comfort required and to create the homelike ambiance whilst acknowledging that the building is home to seriously ill people and allowing the nursing staff to provide the necessary care.

The ability for family members and other loved ones to socialize with the patients is an essential component of hospice care, and the hospice building is a place where family members, including children, should feel free to come and go as they please – as they would in their home.

They need areas where social activities can take place, where they can relax, play games, cook and eat together, and be provided with sleeping accommodations for those who wish to remain overnight.

Care must also be taken to give both patients and family members the opportunity for privacy they require.

Single rooms with an attached bathroom offer the most privacy for both the patient and for family members by their bedside. Having separate sleeping accommodations available nearby for family members ensures privacy for both parties should they require it.

During the initial feasibility phase of a proposed hospice building, the following questions need to be answered to narrow down the scope of the project.

■ What type of service will be offered?

In-patient
- Respite Care
- Symptom Control
- Terminal Care
- Residential Care

Day Care

Home Care

■ How large should the facility be?
What is the required nurse/patient ratio?
How many beds can the area support?

■ What will the length of stay be?

■ Will there be conference facilities?

■ Will there be education facilities?

■ What types of complementary therapies will be offered?

■ What types of counseling services will be offered?

■ What should be planned for future growth?

■ Might there be a change in current procedures?

■ Will there be a sanctuary? – and an office for the chaplains?

■ Will the administrative offices be on- or off-site?

**Services:**

■ Laundry
In house or contracted?
Bed linens, sleepwear/clothes, guest laundry, aromatherapy towels, kitchen and bath towels, etc.

■ Cleaning
In-house or contracted?

■ Cooking
For whom?
Day care center, patients, guests, staff, seminar or conference participants?

■ Grounds keeping
In-house or contracted?

■ Maintenance
In-house or contracted?

# HOSPICE DESIGN MANUAL

## Design Ideals

My discussions with hospice staff from many in-patient hospices led to what they would like to see in their idea of a perfect hospice building.

The list includes:

- An abundance of natural light

- Cozy – careful use of color and textiles

- Non-institutional feel (yet hygienic) – strike the balance!

- Sunny bedrooms with shade and outdoor access

- No long straight corridors

- Use of courtyards – bring in more light and interest

- Site layout so guests and services don't mix (especially the funeral director's vehicle)

- Private rooms, each with private bathroom

- In larger buildings – visual connectors

- Water features

- Direct path to bereavement suite for relatives of deceased

- Easy access to the in-patient facility for day care patients and staff

**The size of a future hospice building will be determined by several factors.**

### Local and State Regulations

Individual states, depending on how the facility will be licensed, may require a specific ratio of nurses to patients.

If, for example, an individual state requires one nurse and a nursing assistant for every six patients (which is typical) then it makes sense to plan the hospice in multiples of six.

For example, a 12 bed unit can be built with possibilities to expand to 18 or 24. In this case a 10- or 11-bed unit would be feasible but, a 13-bed one would not, as the extra bed would require two extra staff.

### Feasibility Studies

Proposed in-patient hospices should conduct feasibility studies of the area's demographics, death rate and other statistics to determine the number of beds are needed.

Other areas of study should include physician and community support and a financial feasibility study.

### Budget

The cost and availability of land and buildings, along with other aspects such as generous donations, will have an impact on the size of the hospice and thus on the services offered.

### Room Sizes

The specific sizes of all the various rooms and areas within the hospice will depend on the number of beds provided. For example, a kitchen for a 16-bed facility will need to be bigger than for an eight-bed facility.

# Hospice Design Manual

## Time Line

**Traveling from an initial dream to a finished hospice building is a step by step process:**

1. Formation of a building committee within the local hospice group

2. Conducting a feasibility study

3. Announce the projects intensions and commencing fund-raising

4. Selecting and engaging an architect, preferably one with hospice design experience

5. Developing a master plan for the hospice using the feasibility study and the architect's experience and research of state and local codes

6. Site evaluation, selection, and purchase

7. Architect to develop a schematic plan

8. Building committee to review initial plans and cost estimates

9. If plans are approved, architect to enter design development phase and complete detailed plans

10. Apply for Certificate of Need (if required)

11. Building committee to review plans as a committee and with board of directors

12. If plans are approved, architect to obtain necessary permits

13. Architect to prepare construction documents – drawings and specifications, including engineering plans prepared by an engineer

14. Notification in local papers of intent to put the project out to bid

15. Contractors obtain construction documents to prepare bid estimates

16. Contractors return bids, which are opened together and reviewed

17. Finalize financing arrangements

18. Contractor selection and drawing up of contract, if bids are acceptable

19. Building commences

20. Begin hiring prospective staff

21. Construction progress reviewed on regular basis with payment given to contractor for completed work.

22. Any changes during the building process will result in change orders which will add to the total cost.

23. Completion of the building shell.

24. Completing the landscaping, and parking, etc.

25. Equipping the building.

26. Complete all staffing.

27. Welcoming the first patients.

Every building project is different, but the above gives a general idea of the order of events.

A major difference between projects is the method of funding. This can range from 100% fund-raised money to 100% bank loan, and will affect the method of payment to the contractor and architect.

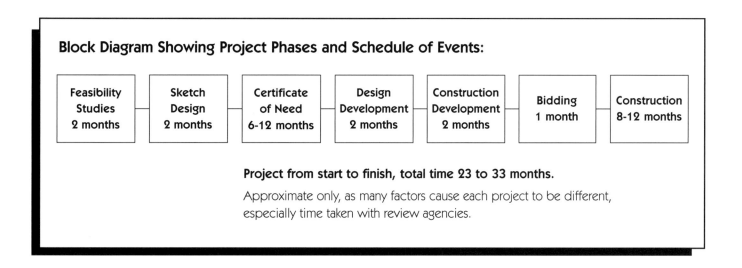

**Block Diagram Showing Project Phases and Schedule of Events:**

| Feasibility Studies 2 months | Sketch Design 2 months | Certificate of Need 6-12 months | Design Development 2 months | Construction Development 2 months | Bidding 1 month | Construction 8-12 months |
|---|---|---|---|---|---|---|

**Project from start to finish, total time 23 to 33 months.**

Approximate only, as many factors cause each project to be different, especially time taken with review agencies.

# Hospice Design Manual

## Site Selection

**Site selection encompasses several aspects, and the selection process should involve the architect.**

### General location
The site should be central to the proposed service area, be easy to find and to access by vehicle, and be close to public transportation if possible.

### Suitability
A feasibility study should be prepared to evaluate the ability of the site to accommodate the requirements a hospice will place on it.

These requirements include:

- Adequate space for parking and vehicular movement including emergency services

- Room on the site to separate public areas from service areas

- Ability to locate patient rooms with a view and sunlight

- Ability to provide privacy to patient rooms

- Space enough to allow for future expansion

- Suitable topography

- If an on-site sewage system is required the site should have appropriate soils and the space required (taking into account future expansion)

- Cost

- Will zoning requirements allow planning permission to be granted for such a project?

- Are there noisy activities nearby? – Airport, factory, gravel pit, etc.

- Will residential neighbors object?

The specific site will greatly influence the design of the hospice. The site should be selected and preferably purchased before design work commences. *(see Site Impact, Section 2, page 26)*

## Users of a Hospice Building

The people who will use a hospice can be divided into two major groups:

- Non-staff members
- Staff members

These two groups can be further subdivided:

### Non Staff –

- Patients
- Family members, friends, and caregivers
- Visitors

### Staff –

- In-patient nursing staff
- Doctors, therapists, and consultants
- Administrative staff
- Home nursing staff
- Maintenance, cleaning, kitchen, and laundry staff (service staff)

Each of these groups of people who use a hospice has different requirements and items of importance to ensure their comfort within the building.

### Patients –

Patients are the reason for the existence of the hospice, but in reality they seldom see much of the building other than the patient area, and often they will not leave their room.

Every effort should therefore be made to ensure the patients' comfort within their rooms.

### Ideally, each patient room should have:

- Sunlight at some point in the day, with protection from glare
- Low window sills allowing the patient to see outside from the bed
- A pleasant view
- Comfortable and adjustable heating/ventilation and lighting
- Access to the outside
- Plenty of room for family members to visit, without feeling cramped
- Easy access within the patient area to other spaces the patient may use – living room, hair salon, etc.
- Plenty of room for nursing procedures
  *(see Patient Room, Section 4, page 72)*

### Family members, friends and caregivers –

These people often benefit more than the patients from the overall appearance and comfort of the hospice.

Suffering through the loss of a loved one or close friend and the subsequent grief, these people need the building to comfort and cosset them.

The building needs to have an intimate sense of scale, should not to appear institutional and should be simple in its layout, making it easy for them to find their way around.

## Users of a Hospice Building *(continued)*

The external appearance of the building and approach to it (the first impression) is of particular importance.

People need to feel comfortable in being able to come and go as they please and have all the rooms they will be using close at hand.

These rooms include:

- Bathrooms with showers
- Snack area
- Quiet room(s)
- Phone room
- Living room
- Sleeping accommodation
- Gardens

### Visitors –

Visitors to hospice who are not family members or friends tend to be visiting the administration, or touring the facility.

The reception is the important space for them – walking in, explaining their business to someone at a reception desk or reception area, and having a comfortable place to wait, with a convenient bathroom.

### Staff Members –

For all members of staff, whether kitchen workers, executives, or nursing aides, the environment in which they work must surely affect their contentment and hence their productivity. This will ripple down and affect the patients directly.

Ensuring that **all** staff members receive a quality environment in which to perform their tasks is of great importance.

Most important is the provision of windows and the ability of all staff members to be able to see outdoors, to be able to see what the weather is doing and when it gets dark, etc. Night staff will feel less isolated being able to see car headlights approaching and be able to witness the beauty of dawn, etc.

Windowless rooms and their reliance on artificial light and ventilation are the most unpleasant space in any building and are best not to be used for work spaces but reserved for storage, bathrooms and the like.

### Medical and Nursing Staff –

Whilst for non-staff members the aesthetics and 'home-like' quality of the building are of prime importance, the nursing and medical staff are looking for an environment in which they can efficiently work. They are taking care of seriously ill people and need all the help they can get through efficient design, and pleasant work areas.

Important considerations include:

- Short corridor runs
- Nurses' station central to the patient area
- Areas of privacy – distinct 'staff only' areas
- A staff break room away from the patient area with facilities to shower and change
- Adequate and convenient storage

## Users of a Hospice Building *(continued)*

- Windows in all work spaces
- Easy access to all the other spaces which get used by patients
- Bright, pleasant exam/consult/therapy rooms.
- Choices of materials that allow easy cleaning and the ability to easily move patients and equipment through the area

### Administrative Staff –

The 'admin area' requires the dichotomy of good communications within the area, and private spaces. Open-plan admin offices have been shown not to work. However, a balance can be achieved by having private, personal office spaces but not isolating them and allowing communications between them – by using a semi open plan form, or by combining small open plan areas and private offices.

Plenty of natural light in all areas will help create a pleasant work area.

### Service Staff –

The need for windows in both the kitchen and laundry areas is commonly overlooked. If possible both areas should be located on outside walls to allow natural light into the spaces. Special attention should be paid to the air handling in the kitchen to ensure that this area does not get too hot and unpleasant to work in.

# HOSPICE DESIGN MANUAL

## Zones Within The Hospice

**A larger, full-service hospice building will comprise several distinct zones:**

- Entrance and public area – reception, quiet room, sanctuary, chaplains' office, dining room, bathrooms, and consulting rooms for social workers and counselors

- Patient area – patient rooms, bathrooms, treatment and exam rooms, nurses' station, storage, utility rooms, living room, quiet rooms, therapy rooms hair salon, and medication room

- Service areas – kitchen, laundry rooms, storage, mechanical room, and bathrooms

- Administrative area – offices for managers, assistants, fund-raisers, volunteer coordinator, and home hospice staff. Bathrooms and storage

- Classroom and conference facilities, bathrooms and storage

- Day care center

The first four zones are required of any hospice. The last two can either be added as the hospice program grows, or included at the onset

## Problems With Existing Hospices

Almost all the recommendations in this manual came about because they were lacking in one or more of the hospices visited during the research. The following, in no particular order, is a list of the most commonly found problems:

- Again and again – not enough storage space – especially for large items such as wheelchairs, hoists, etc.

- Location of the living room precludes its use. A living room can be a very important part of the hospice, but it needs to be next to the patient area if it is to be used

- Patient rooms with patio doors but with thresholds too high to wheel a bed over

- Patient rooms overlooking the funeral director's arrival area

- Long corridors. (Hard on nurses and give an institutional feel)

- Difficulty finding the main entrance when approaching the building

- Lack of visual connectors, making it hard to find one's way around, and/or confusing floor plans

- Lack of a discreet system of transferring deceased patients to funeral home. The following should be avoided:
  - ☐ through main entry
  - ☐ through door adjacent to main entry
  - ☐ through service area, next to the dumpsters
  - ☐ through reception area

- Institutional feel overall

- Lack of designated smoking area, or smoking area too close to patient area, causing an odor problem

- Open-plan admin areas – noisy with no privacy

- North-facing patient rooms, receiving little sunshine

- Rooms such as the hair salon added as an afterthought, often into windowless rooms

- No electrically operated doors, especially at patient entry

- Lighting too bright with no dimming switches provided

- Skylights without blinds – too bright

- Poor positioning of mirrors in bathrooms

- No telephone available for family members

## Problems With Existing Hospices *(continued)*

- No seating in reception area, or reception area too large and impersonal

- Too few, or no counseling and consulting rooms

- Family suites located too far from patient area and not used, and/or not handicapped accessible

- Poor kitchen location causing long travel path to and from patient rooms

- Providing only showers or only tubs

- No windows in sanctuary, nurses' station, staff offices, quiet rooms, and work areas

- No separation between clean and dirty areas (For example, food going one way down a corridor and dirty linen coming the other way.)

- No staff break room, or the one provided is unpleasant (no windows, too small, etc.)

- Patient bedrooms for two patients – just doesn't work

- Call lights set in recesses and not visible from corridor

- No privacy for nurses, doctors, and other professionals. No quiet, private area to write notes

- Patient beds arranged in the room so a nurse cannot see the patients from the door

- Sanctuary located next to a noisy area

- Classroom(s), day care center, admin areas too small

- Light fixtures too high and hard to reach when changing light bulbs

- Staff changing/locker rooms not provided or inadequate

- Ceiling hoist fastened in the wrong locations and unusable

- Large 'shopping-mall' type parking lots

- No bathrooms near conference room/classrooms

- Night entry too far from nurses' station

- Areas in the hospice not handicapped accessible

- No private space for relatives, and/or too few quiet rooms

- High windowsills in patient rooms

- Specially equipped bathrooms too far from patient rooms and not used

# HOSPICE DESIGN MANUAL

## Section 2

# HOSPICE DESIGN MANUAL

## Accessibility

Hospices need to be fully barrier-free to ADA (Americans with Disabilities Act) standards to allow full use by any staff members and visitors who have restricted mobility, and of course, by patients. This includes barrier-free access into the building from all parking areas.

Grade access into the building should be provided and an elevator provided to access any other levels.

If patients are to be housed on different levels the elevator should be large enough to accommodate a patient's gurney and attendants.

Handrails should be placed along all corridors in the patient areas.

All bathrooms should be accessible, and patient baths should also be designed to allow nursing staff to fully assist the patient. *(see Patient Bathroom, Section 4, page 73)*

Any doorways used while transporting patients should have a minimum opening of 3-foot 8-inches. A 3-foot door with a 1-foot opening side panel works well.

Electrically operated doors should be incorporated into corridors where nurses will be pushing patients around in a wheelchair (for example between the patient area and the living room). Otherwise patients end up being pulled backward through doors.

Electric front doors ease the arrival of patients.

All signage in the building should include sensory/braille lettering.

In areas with significant ethnic populations multilingual signage should be considered. For example, many areas have a large Spanish-speaking population.

With the exception of non-skid entry mats, throw and scatter rugs should not be used anywhere in the building.

In climate zones which experience snow and ice, heated exterior walkways should be considered, especially at the main entrance.

## Alarm Systems and Security

With the increase in prescription drug abuse and its associated theft, security is important for a hospice building.

Areas of the hospice building unused at night should have the capability of being separated with lockable doors from those areas in use.

These areas would include:

- administrative and other office areas
- day care center
- commercial kitchen areas
- classroom/conference room(s)

These unused areas should also be equipped with motion sensors.

All exterior doors and windows should be connected to an alarm system, including all patio doors off the patient rooms. These patio doors, if used, should each have an individual alarm at the nurses' station indicating which door is open.

Visiting family members should be asked to use the night entrance and not the patient's patio door.

All entrances but especially the night entrance used by family members should be designed in such a way that makes it difficult for someone to conceal themselves.

The night entrance should also be equipped with a closed circuit TV monitor connected to the nurses' station, and the nurses should be able to open the door with remote lock activation. (buzzer system).

At night after the cleaning staff leave, the only staff in the building will usually be nurses. Consideration should be given to installing a panic alarm button for these nurses, connected to the local police department.

The mechanical system should have an alarm to notify staff and the heating company if there is an equipment failure, especially with the heating plant, so repairs can be made before the temperature drops.

A fire alarm system should be installed as per local and state codes, connected directly to the local fire department.

# HOSPICE DESIGN MANUAL

## Body and Spirit

Another important aspect of good hospice care is caring for the patients' minds and spirits as well as their body – looking after their spiritual needs as well as the more apparent physical requirements.

Patients' family members and friends also have similar needs.

The architecture of a building can play a large part in this aspect of design. This can range from designing a patient room so that it may easily become personalized (e.g., by providing suitable shelving to display personal items) to the overall design in allowing the building to cosset and shelter whilst maintaining a strong connection to the outdoors and surrounding nature.

The following are some of the design elements which can aid in comforting the spirit as well as the body:

■ Creating a variety of cozy spaces, some to allow socialization and some to allow privacy. A fireplace with its flickering flames in the living room will attract people and encourage friendships. *(see Living Rooms, Section 4, page 76)*

■ Taking as much advantage as possible of natural light and views, allowing light to enter the building from different directions, along with windows that open to allow fresh air and sounds to enter. Placing the windows to maximize the views.

■ Providing a place for children to play freely under supervision, whilst not disturbing those wishing to rest.

■ Incorporating water features and art works in the design. *(see Water Features, Section 2, page 47 and Works of Art, Section 2, page 48)*

■ Using natural or minimally processed building materials to minimize the release of toxic chemicals *(see Environmental Considerations, Section 2, page 26)*

■ Making sure the direction of travel throughout the building is clear with a gentle progression from public areas through to semi-public areas and to the private rooms.

■ Avoiding long corridors, utilizing different corridor widths with recesses and nooks for plants or artworks, and using gentle changes in direction.

■ Using recessed entries into rooms, thus making the entry into the room less abrupt.

## Building Exterior

A hospice is different from most other buildings in that the architecture needs to comfort and reassure both patients and visitors.

This needs to be accomplished with the first impression, upon arrival, with the exterior, and then throughout the building on the inside.

The exterior architecture should have an intimate sense of scale. The building is a facility for the caring of seriously ill people and will have features necessary to accomplish its mission, such as a large covered entrance to allow patients to enter from ambulances in inclement weather.

But with careful design the building's mass and its detailing can soften an otherwise large and institutional looking building.

One important factor in making someone more comfortable when approaching and entering a building is to make every step of the way as clear as possible – no wondering where to go – which can be unsettling.

Four stages of approaching a building for a visitor –

■ **Turning off the main road into the hospice grounds:**

The sign will be the first impression and should be visible from both directions. It should not be too corporate looking – i.e., not too large and flashy but just enough to convey the name and location.

■ **Arriving at the building and finding a place to park:**

The building will become visible, and here the exterior architecture of the building is of prime importance. A large open parking lot has little appeal and feels very commercial/institutional. Far better are smaller groups of parking spaces with landscaping in between, and paved footpaths leading to the entrance.

■ **Approaching the building on foot:**

Here as one approaches the building the first impression is really formed – the appearance and details of the building. It should be clear as to where the entrance is.

## Building Exterior *(continued)*

### ■ Entering the building:

The important factor here is making a comfortable transition from the outside to the inside – helped by a covered entry, keeping an intimate sense of scale, and upon entering having it be obvious where to proceed in the building. A covered porch with a rocking chair provides a place for someone to sit and gather themselves before entry.

The object of the approach is to set a comfortable feel before entering the building. All four steps need to work and need full consideration for a successful project.

Patients themselves also need to be comforted and reassured by the architecture, but if arriving by ambulance they will miss the first three steps, and their first impression will be of the front entrance.

It is important for this reason that the patients enter from an ambulance through the front door, or a separate but appealingly designed designated ambulance entry.

It is most important that the ambulance entry is not 'round back' through the service area.

The 'emergency room' type of entry should be avoided.

Patients require a non-institutional design so they don't feel as if they are entering a hospital, and need to feel reassured that they are entering a facility which can and will take good care of them.

## Courtyards

The use of courtyards is a valuable tool for hospice design.

Courtyards bring natural daylight into the building and provide interest to what would otherwise be internal spaces. They also provide visual connectors, making a large building less confusing to a visitor.

A courtyard may be large and accessed by users of the hospice, or smaller with no access:

- Accessed courtyards may be used for sitting in the sun, out of the wind, or for taking a stroll, and they can include a terrace connected to the dining area or other interior space. They also allow patients with dementia to walk outside without fear of them leaving the area.

- Enclosed courtyards are usually smaller and can be landscaped with rocks and water features.

Courtyards can be as effective if open on one side as they can if fully enclosed, but with an enclosed courtyards thought must be given to how to access it for maintenance, and what equipment may be required, such as a lawn mower.

The geographical location is an important consideration since it would be unwise to create a small enclosed courtyard in an area which regularly receives a large amount of snow.

# HOSPICE DESIGN MANUAL

## Emergency Generator

An emergency generator with an automatic transfer switch should be provided.

Generators come large enough to power up the entire facility during a power outage but as a minimum they should be large enough to provide power to any equipment vital to life safety.

This would include:

- Nurse call system
- Fire alarm system
- Sprinkler pump
- Elevator (if used to transport patients)
- Telephone system
- Sewage pump
- Central oxygen system

Emergency lighting and exit signs should have battery backup.

All emergency lighting should be on dedicated circuits.

## Entrances

Several entrances will be required (although some may be combined):

- Main Entrance – Used by administrative staff, nursing and medical staff, patients, and visitors.

- Service Entrance – Used for all deliveries: food, equipment, supplies, laundry, and to access the dumpsters and oxygen bottles if so supplied.

- Night Entrance – Used by visiting loved ones and relatives after the main doors are closed for the day, and by night nursing staff.

- Funeral Director's Entrance – Used by funeral directors to transport deceased patients.

- Patio Entrances – Patio doors off patient rooms and other areas such as living rooms to access the gardens and patios used by patients and their visitors.

The main entrance, service entrance, and funeral director's entrance require vehicular access, with any canopies high enough to accommodate an ambulance (with its rack of lights) and service vehicles.

The main entrance and the night entrance require close proximity to parking.

Electrically operated doors for the patient entry greatly assist those bringing a patient into the facility.

The building may also need additional doors for use as fire escapes as required by egress codes.

Installing radiant heat tubing under the entry walkway greatly enhances safety during the winter months in areas receiving snow and ice.

*(see Building Exterior, Section 2, page 21; Reception, Section 4, page 88; Alarm Systems and Security, Section 2, page 19)*

# Hospice Design Manual

## Environmental Considerations

A building devoted to taking care of seriously ill people should provide as healthy an environment as possible.

### A healthy environment would include:

- No toxic materials used in construction
- Providing natural light and ventilation for patients and staff
- Energy efficiency throughout
- Careful noise control
- Even, comfortable heat and air conditioning with a thermostat in each patient room
- Use of natural fabrics

The hospice is a perfect building to design in an environmentally friendly fashion. This can improve working conditions, increase comfort for the patients, and lessen the impact of the building upon the Earth.

By providing natural light and ventilation to most spaces, the spaces are much more pleasant to be in; patients will be comfortable, staff happier and there will be less demand on electricity to illuminate dark internal spaces during daytime.

The U.S. Green Building Council's Leadership in Energy and Environmental Design program (LEED) publishes extensive design guidelines and workshops for designing sustainable buildings, and provides information to maximize building performance through environmental strategies. They also offer a certification process. It is their goal to save the planet "one building at a time".

It is highly recommended that all new hospices be LEED certified. (www.usgbc.org/LEED) The following is a brief synopsis of the LEED guidelines, along with a few other considerations.

### SITE IMPACT

Every effort should be made to reduce the building's impact upon the site.

### 1) Storm water runoff:

Storm water runoff into existing streams creates problems with aquatic life. Government studies estimate that 70% of pollution of inland waters is carried by storm water.

Solutions to storm water runoff:

- Use of bioretention cells, otherwise known as 'raingardens'. These represent an infiltration technique designed to absorb and filter storm water from impervious surfaces such as roofs and parking lots. They keep the water where it falls, slowly releasing it. They are small ecological systems which demonstrate how careful land-scaping combined with engineering can protect the ecosystem
- Use of porous pavement systems in areas of lower use such as access roads and extra parking allowing rain to infiltrate the ground
- Use of retention ponds

Erosion and sediment control should be managed carefully during construction.

## Environmental Considerations (continued)

### 2) Light pollution

Utilize efficient external lighting whilst improving night sky access and lessening the impact for nocturnal animals. This can be accomplished by using shielded lights to direct the light downward, reducing the brightness of the lights, minimizing the lighting of landscape features, minimizing the use of architectural floodlighting and signage lighting, and by using the least amount of light necessary for safety and security.

A professional lighting designer can help with these goals.

### 3) Heat island effect

Heat islands are created where there are large temperature differences between the building and parking and surrounding areas.

Heat islands cause internal temperatures to rise requiring more energy to keep the building cool.

The heat island effect can be mitigated by the use of deciduous tree plantings around the building to provide shade in summer (whilst allowing solar gain to the building in winter), by creating smaller parking areas broken up with vegetation rather than having the 'sea of parking,' and by the use in general of light colored materials.

### 4) Other considerations

Minimizing site disturbance reduces plant and wildlife habitat destruction. The greater the building density on the site the greater the damage will be to the local ecology. Care should be taken not to disrupt wildlife migration routes.

A site which can be accessed by public transportation is preferable to one which cannot (all other factors being equal).

Sometimes parking can be shared with a neighboring building to reduce the amount needed.

Providing a bicycle parking area and bicycle paths on the site encourages the use of non-motorized transport.

### WATER EFFICIENCY

Using water efficiency measures can reduce water usage in a building by up to 30%.

Principal methods are:

- Using low-flow fixtures
- Using automatic controls
- Using captured rainwater for landscape watering

More complex systems use rainwater for toilet flushing, requiring a separate plumbing system.

### ENERGY and ATMOSPHERE

Energy consumption can easily be reduced by economical and readily available practices, which in turn reduce atmospheric pollution from power plants.

## Environmental Considerations *(continued)*

These practices include:

- Use of insulated glazing
- Providing good insulation
- Use of daylight with windows but also with sun tubes and fiber-optic devices
- Use of passive solar techniques such as creating a thermal mass and capturing solar heat gain in winter, and orienting the building with regard to sunlight and wind patterns
- Optimizing the heating, ventilation and air-conditioning (HVAC) system
- Use of compact fluorescent lights
- Use of trees and overhangs for shade
- Use of LED emergency lighting
- Use of windows which open for ventilation
- Use of light colors

On-site creation of renewable energy is more and more feasible using solar power, wind power, and biomass systems.

'Green power' through the grid is now readily available. A contract is signed to purchase a portion of the electricity used from renewable sources.

Ozone protection is an important consideration. Using CFC-free equipment protects the ozone layer. Servicing and updating refrigeration systems regularly helps minimize CFC release.

### RECYCLING and BUILDING CONSTRUCTION

Recycling reduces the generation of waste to go to landfills or incinerators both during construction and once the building is occupied.

During construction much of the construction waste can be recycled or reused. This includes lumber, cardboard, and gypsum products. Many building products are available which do not use all virgin materials but have a recycled content.

The use of materials extracted and manufactured in the region prevents materials from being trucked all across the country.

Many products are available which are manufactured from rapidly renewable materials.

These products include:

- Composite panels made from wheat fiber
- Bamboo flooring
- Cotton batt insulation
- Sunflower seed board

The use of certified wood ensures all lumber used during the project comes from forests harvested with environmentally responsible forestry practices.

Once the building becomes occupied paper, corrugated cardboard, glass, plastics, and metals can all be recycled. Recycling becomes more effective if convenient recycling facilites are readily available to all occupants of the building.

## Environmental Considerations *(continued)*

### AIR QUALITY

Most people spend 90% of their time indoors. Pollutants tend to be two to five times higher inside than out making the quality of the indoor environment a high priority in any building.

A coordinated approach is required between the architect and the HVAC engineer to ensure that fresh-air intakes are away from vehicular areas, toilet vents, smoking areas, etc.

Any internal smoking area should have a separate ventilation system.

A new system should be thoroughly flushed out to eliminate contaminants prior to occupancy and should include an air monitoring system for carbon monoxide and radon.

Materials containing VOCs (volatile organic compounds) should be eliminated from the construction where possible. These include composite wood products, certain carpeting and certain adhesives and sealants. These will 'out-gas' VOCs and will especially react to sunlight.

Photo-copying and fax machines are a source of indoor chemicals and along with cleaning cupboards should be isolated from the main ventilation system and be provided with a separate ventilation system.

Heating, ventilation, and lighting systems should be provided with a high flexibility of control to provide energy savings and to provide a high degree of comfort, which will in turn promote productivity.

The HVAC system should also provide humidity control, as air that is too dry creates static, and air that is too moist promotes the growth of mold.

# HOSPICE DESIGN MANUAL

## Fire Protection

The National Fire Protection Association (NFPA) Life Safety Code requires that all hospices have sprinkler systems installed. Some locations especially in rural areas may have local/state codes requiring water storage capabilities for the sprinkler system in addition to hook-up points for fire trucks. A separate room will be required to house the sprinkler system in these cases.

The sprinkler pump should be connected to an emergency generator which should start up automatically in the event of power loss.

The fire alarm system should be connected directly to the local fire department, to ensure the fastest possible response, and should also be connected to the emergency generator.

A fire alarm which sounds gongs or chimes is far less alarming for patients than horns or bells.

Hospices using town water supplies should have hydrants located on-site, to cover the entire building.

The site layout should be designed to ensure that fire and other emergency vehicles have the room required to maneuver.

The building should be designed and built to the current NFPA 101 Life Safety Code standards. These address means of egress, methods of fire protection, materials to be used, fire compartmentalization, sprinkler requirements, etc.

Fire and safety issues should be considered early in the design process, with input from the fire marshal's office.

As well as obtaining a construction permit from the local or state fire marshal's office the hospice will be required to have a written plan detailing the actions to be taken in the case of a fire emergency.

Opinions differ greatly on the type of flooring to be used in the patient area. Certain hospice managers insist on carpeted floors, whilst others insist on vinyl tile.

There are certainly pros and cons to both. The main reason for choosing carpeting is that it is non-institutional looking and the main reason for choosing vinyl is that it is easier to keep clean.

■ Vinyl floors
  – make it easier to wheel wheelchairs etc
  – are noisy and slippery
  – look institutional
  – are easier to clean up after a spill

■ Carpeting
  – can show stains
  – makes it harder to push wheelchairs etc.
  – makes it harder to control infection
  – creates a homelike atmosphere
  – is quieter, especially in hallways

New low-pile, solution-dyed fiberglass carpeting may have solved the problems associated with carpeting. Low pile makes it easier to wheel something over, and fiberglass cannot stain.

Carpet tiles allow for easy replacement but if used should be specifically manufactured for use in health care facilties.

New wood-grained vinyl floors look more attractive than traditional vinyl flooring.

Laminate flooring is an option for the public areas but as it is not seamless, it is unsuitable for patient areas.

Several hospices use carpeting in all areas other than patient rooms and bathrooms and in those rooms use vinyl, and several hospices use carpeting throughout.

Whichever type of flooring is selected it must be of the highest quality and suitable for the medical environment.

# Hospice Design Manual

## Future Development and Expansion

As the hospice movement grows, new hospice buildings will be built around the country. As the services offered by each hospice develop and grow, the buildings will need to be expanded to provide the additional services required.

Formulating a master plan and designing a building with possibilities for growth is therefore very important.

Careful thought should be given at the onset as to what services are to be provided now and in the future. What will be needed to provide those services?

Will extra accommodation be required and if so, how will it join up to the existing building?

Where possible interior spaces should not be too 'over designed' and have the flexibility to change uses.

*For example: The Peace Hospice in Watford, England, built a two story building and finished off the first floor. When the need arises, the second floor can be finished off to double the size of the existing building from a 12-bed to a 24-bed facility. Each floor will have a self-contained patient area. The existing kitchen and other back-up areas were designed to be large enough at the start to be sufficient for the expansion.*

Several hospices have an additional wing planned, connecting near the nurses' station, requiring only extra bedrooms, and utilizing all the existing facilities.

Care should be taken that the other rooms in the hospice will remain large enough with such an expansion – especially the kitchen, because regulations may require a commercial kitchen if more beds are added.

Planning ahead should also include looking at the services – size of septic system, heating and ventilating equipment, electrical entrance, etc.

In addition to more patient rooms, future development may include the addition of extra services – physical therapy, a day care center, a children's play area, additional counseling rooms, an education center, etc.

## Gardens and Landscaping

The grounds surrounding a stand-alone hospice play an important part in the overall hospice experience.

Having a pleasant view from the patients' rooms and other common areas such as the living room is important to assist in maintaining a calm state of mind.

A landscaped garden using either existing trees or plantings or starting from scratch should be part of every project's budget. Even small spaces can be carefully treated to become areas of natural beauty and a joy to the eye.

Paths around the gardens are nice but in reality are seldom used by patients – they are used primarily by family members and visitors if at all. If paths are to be used, they should be hard surfaced to facilitate wheelchairs and to minimize the treading-in of gravel.

Birds fascinate many bed-bound people, and a nicely landscaped area combined with feeders readily attracts them, providing hours of interest for patients.

Raised planters at the side of patios allow patients who use wheelchairs to tend a few flowers. These can be located on the patio areas off the day care center, living room, and patient rooms.

A small private garden for contemplation is a wonderful addition to a sanctuary or bereavement suite.

Gardens can be anything from formal affairs designed on an axis with waterfalls and fountains to a simple, random collection of trees with daffodils and other seasonal flowers. Either one will serve the purpose.

If the hospice is to have grounds keepers as part of the staff, then storage space will need to be allotted or a separate building will be required to store all the yard tools and planting equipment.

If the grounds keeping work is to be contracted out, then the road layout will need to allow room for a landscapers' truck and trailer to be parked all day and not be in the way.

Exterior hose connections will be required, and in certain climates a watering system will have to be considered.

Landscaping can also be used to shield the hospice from such as noisy roads with high-density plantings or by building a landscaped earthen berm.

Exterior electrical outlets should be provided for a multitude of uses from Christmas lights to small entertainment and PA systems.

## Infection Control

The control of infectious disease within the hospice is essential for the protection of patients, staff, family members, and visitors.

Infection can be controlled by preventing cross-contamination, by providing materials and finishes which can easily be cleaned and sterilized, by ensuring contaminated air isn't returned to the building, and possibly by providing an isolation room.

### Cross-contamination:

Patient bathrooms should be for patient use only. Staff should use staff bathrooms, and visitors and family members should be provided with public bathrooms close by.

Hand sanitizers should be readily available in all bathrooms.

All cutlery and dishes should be sterilized with hot water (to at least 160°F) during the dishwashing process.

### Materials and finishes:

Patient rooms have to be thoroughly cleaned especially between patients, so all surfaces should be easily sanitized.

Vinyl flooring in the patient rooms is the easiest to keep clean and is the material of choice for many hospices. However, it can have an institutional feel to it as well as being noisier and more slippery than carpet.

New types of flooring which resemble hardwood flooring are the most successful.

Carpet has a more homelike appeal, softens sound, and is easier under feet.

If carpeting is to be used, it has to be of the highest quality and be designed for medical facilities. These are fully sealed (rubber backed) and solution dyed. New fiberglass carpeting is fully stain-proof. *(see Flooring, Section 2, page 31)*

### Isolation Rooms:

There are several different levels in providing an isolation room.

At the simplest level the room maintains a negative air pressure, creating a reverse air flow ensuring that air enters the room only from the rest of the patient area.

In the next level, along with the reverse air flow, a small vestibule is provided as one enters and leaves the room, which can be separate from the regular room entrance. The vestibule contains a sink and counter to enable nursing and medical staff to thoroughly sanitize before re-entering the patient area.

The final method which guarantees isolation is to enter the patient's room via an anteroom. This is similar to a vestibule and also equipped with a sink and counter, but upon entering, both doors lock and the room undergoes an air change (taking about 30 seconds). The same procedure occurs on leaving.

The anteroom is the only way into the room for staff and visitors. It is generally unnecessary to install such a system unless it is fairly certain that highly infectious patients will be admitted.

## Lighting

Providing an abundance of natural light during daylight hours will have a positive effect on all the building's occupants. Of equal importance is the quality of artificial lighting provided.

Patient rooms will require an especially flexible lighting scheme - dim lighting for periods of relaxation, task lighting for activities such as reading, and brighter lighting for a physician or nurse to conduct an examination, with care to have no lights shining into the patient's eyes.

An important consideration for the overall lighting scheme is to limit the types of lightbulbs required so that staff members don't have to stock a multitude of different bulbs and have to puzzle out which goes where.

Good exterior lighting is important since hospices can be targets for break-ins – there should be no dark corners or unlit areas.

The night entrance should be especially well lit to provide security for the nursing staff. All driveways and parking areas should be well lit.

All exterior lighting should be controlled with light-sensitive controls and not timers to ensure continuous operation as darkness falls.

Recessed down lights and wall sconces are preferred to fluorescent tube fixtures.

Lightbulbs that cast light in the warm spectrum are prefered. *(see Use of Color, Section 2, page 46)*

## Mechanical Systems

The size and requirements of a heating/cooling system will vary among hospices depending on the hospice size and climate zone.

Careful design can take advantage of the warmth and light from the sun to reduce the heating/lighting requirements.

Regardless of the specific heating/cooling system it is essential to have an adequate hot water supply to the entire building 24 hours a day.

Some state and local codes will stipulate requirements.

*For example North Carolina requires the following:*

- *Patient rooms – 6.5 gallons per hour per bed with a temperature of 110°F – 116°F*

- *Kitchen/Laundry – 4.0 gallons per hour per bed with a temperature of 140°F*

Patient rooms should have individual thermostats adjustable between 65°F and 80°F

All hospices should be equipped with air handling and air conditioning systems.

The used linen room, dirty utility room, bathrooms and custodians' closets should all have negative pressure in relationship to adjacent areas.

The clean linen room, clean utility room, and medication room should all have positive pressure in relationship to adjacent areas.

All other areas should have neutral pressure.

If desired, oxygen can be provided to the bedside in three different ways –

■ **Piped in-wall:**

Piped-in oxygen is the most convenient and a console next to the bed connecting to oxygen, air, and suction is a great help to nursing staff.

It can be supplied from one of two sources:

☐ **from tanks –**

Tanks need to be changed frequently by trained personnel from the supplier and be checked on a regular basis to prevent running out. Tanks need to be located in a secure storage area outside with room for full and empty tanks and good access for delivery vehicles.

☐ **from farms –**

Oxygen farms are on-site facilities that provide and store all the oxygen the facility will need. They consist of the oxygen-producing equipment coupled to a large tank surrounded on three sides by a masonry wall. The farm needs to be a minimum of 50 feet from the building for safety and security and to be sensitively located on the site (avoiding an eyesore). It must comply with any state or local regulations.

Facilities must be provided to change over to a tank system in the event of system failure.

■ **Concentrators:**

Oxygen concentrators are noisy and present a trip hazard with the tubing along the floor and power cord. If used, storage space will be required.

■ **Individual bottles:**

Individual bottles in a cart also present a trip hazard. They require storage space inside for both bottles and carts, and secure external storage for both full and empty bottles.

The bottles don't last long and require frequent changing by nursing staff, who find bottles very heavy to work with.

Some administrations prefer concentrators or bottles, as less oxygen tends to get used than with a piped-in system, but the nursing staff overwhelmingly prefers to work with piped-in oxygen.

If oxygen will be used in any form in a hospice building, then the issue of smoking becomes of vital importance.

If patients are allowed to smoke inside, the smoking room must be located well away from the patient area in a separate fire zone.

The oxygen system needs to be installed in accordance with NFPA 99C and will require appropriate certification.

# Hospice Design Manual

## Parking

Adequate parking is important, and on sites with limited space as many parking spaces as possible will need to be squeezed in.

As a minimum, one space per patient and one space per full-time staff member and half a space per part-time staff member has been suggested. Most areas will have specific numbers required by local codes.

Staff and visitor parking should be located close to the front entrance.

If the night entrance is away from the front, extra parking should be provided close by.

Maintenance staff and contractors may want to use the service entrance, and space should be provided there for them to park.

Care should be taken to avoid the large institutional/ shopping center type of parking lot and split up the parking into smaller groups with connecting paved pathways.

Separating staff and visitor parking helps reduce the 'sea of parking.'

All parking areas and driveways should have adequate illumination, controlled by a light-sensitive device.

Ease and efficiency of snow removal should be taken into account in all areas of the site layout, especially when dividing the parking area into smaller areas.

Careful thought should be applied to the design of the storm drain system. *(see Environmental Considerations, Section 2, page 26)*

The use of a porous pavement system in less-used areas can reduce the storm drain load and also reduce the 'heat island' effect.

In areas not prone to muddy conditions overspill parking can be provided on grass areas.

## Patient Call System

Each patient room, bathroom, and other areas accessible to the patients (dining room, living room, smoking room, etc.) should be equipped with a call system.

The call button should turn on a light above that room's doorway and light up on a panel in the nurses' station, with an accompanying tone to signal the nursing staff through the use of belt pagers.

Any corridor intersections should also have call lights indicating in which direction a nurse should go.

Buzzers in the hallway should be avoided, as they tend to cause anxiety for other patients, but an audible tone on the central panel will direct the nurses' attention to the call.

If the patient's room door is recessed from the corridor, the light should be placed in the corridor instead of over the door so as to be clearly visible from the nurses' station and other areas.

The call system in the patient rooms should allow the patient to hold on to the call switch from their bed. It should be subtly illuminated to help the patient to find it at night.

A system should also be in place for a nurse, after responding to a patient's call, to summon extra help without alarming the patient. This could be a designated wall-mounted call button, a code using the patient's call button, or a button on the nurse's pager.

# HOSPICE DESIGN MANUAL

## Remembrance / Dedication

Areas of the hospice will need to be set aside for remembrance of deceased patients and for dedication to those who donated towards the building of the hospice.

**Remembrance:**

Different methods include:

- Entering the names of the deceased into a large book, often placed on a special table, in an alcove, or in the sanctuary.
- Lighting candles in a loved one's memory. (Fire regulations would most likely insist on electric candles.)
- Engraving the names of the deceased into bricks and placing them into a remembrance pathway outside or onto leaves on a painted tree of life.

**Dedication:**

Acknowledging help towards building the hospice is very important, and is often expected by the donors.

This can range from naming the entire facility for some- one who made it possible, to naming sections of the facility (such as individual rooms) down to a small acknowledgment of some kind.

A common practice is to engrave donor names in a large marble or granite plaque in the reception area. This, however, creates a 'mausoleum' feel immediately upon entry – the opposite effect of what is desired. More subtle approaches convey the thanks just as well and can complement the space.

*For example, the Hospice House in Monterey, California came up with a novel solution, incorporating a track in the corridor handrail assembly into which small painted tiles may be inserted. A local artist glazes the donors name in the tile and they are slid into place. These tiles provide decoration to the corridors, can be easily added at any time, and are a visual statement encouraging others to donate.*

## Remodeling Existing Buildings

Hospices have a large number of specific design requirements, so it is easiest to provide the desired accommodations with new construction.

However, as the demand for new hospices increases, urban areas in particular will have to consider remodeling existing buildings where lack of available land would prohibit new construction.

Great care must be exercised when considering the purchase of an existing building for this purpose since existing buildings should be able to meet all the requirements for a new facility.

The building should be thoroughly evaluated for suitability, and a cost estimate prepared of the proposed conversion to ensure financial realism.

As well as the building's ability to house all the requirements at the outset, thought should be given to possibilities of expanding the building to allow for future growth as the programs develop.

When converting an existing building into a hospice substantial changes should be expected, and every attempt must be made not to compromise the services of the hospice by the constraints applied by the existing building.

Several existing hospices have achieved very successful conversions by studying the problems carefully.

Existing buildings previously used for nursing care are often easier to convert into hospice care than other types of building.

Houses have an advantage of already having a residential feel to them, but the problems faced in making a practical facility should be carefully considered.

If an existing building is donated to the hospice group, the building still needs to be carefully evaluated, and if deemed unsuitable, sold to provide the money to purchase or build a more suitable one.

If the existing building has more than one level, patients should only be located on only one level, as locating patients on two floors places an unacceptable load on the nursing staff. The exception to this would be in a large facility where each floor was a self-contained unit with elevator access to each floor. This would require an elevator large enough to accommodate a bed or gurney and attendants.

Second-floor accommodations should be considered only for non-patient uses – admin, education, conference rooms, home hospice staff, etc.

Any use of a second floor will require an elevator.

## Remodeling Existing Buildings *(continued)*

Every hospice building should be fully accessible.

The most common problems with remodeling are:

- Providing adequately sized rooms which allow full access all around the bed

- Providing accessible and specially equipped bathrooms

- To build doors and corridors of adequate width

- Providing a grade entrance (with no steps)

Windowsills in existing buildings are often too high to allow patients to see out from their beds.

Maintenance costs are often substantially higher with an existing building as opposed to a new one.

When considering 'classic' older buildings for remodeling, care must be taken not to be blinded by the exterior aesthetics if the interior is unsuitable for conversion into a hospice facility.

Specific codes, rules, and regulations vary around the country. These will need thorough research prior to beginning the design, as the building will have to meet all state and local building codes.

Different states license a hospice in different ways, and many states don't have specific licenses for hospices. These states may issue licenses as either congregate, skilled living, acute living or as a nursing home.

Specific licensing requirements will affect the size of a proposed hospice, so early research into these rules is essential.

Most states will require an ADA barrier-free permit and a construction permit from the fire marshal, dealing with fire zones, alarms, construction type, sprinkler systems, and egress issues. This will be based on the NFPA 101 Life Safety Code. (In Maine, for example, the State Fire Marshal will issue a permit based on the requirements for a nursing home.)

Gas and vacuum systems need to be installed in accordance with NFPA 99C.

For example some of the regulations applicable to inpatient hospice buildings in North Carolina are:

- *Ratio of nurses to patients – one RN to six patients*

- *Required minium square feet for dining room – 20 square feet per patient*

- *Required minimum square feet for recreation space – 35 square foot per patient*

- *Required minimum square foot of storage space – 5 square feet per patient*

- *Maximum number of beds before requiring a commercial kitchen – 15 beds*

- *Maximum travel distances for nurses, from bed to nurses' station – 150 feet*

- *Distance of oxygen farm from building – 50 feet minimum*

- *Width of corridors – 8-feet, or 6-feet if doors are recessed to create an 8-by-8-foot area at room entrances*

- *Single door patient egress width – 3-foot 8-inch mininum*

- *Dish water temp – 160°F minimum*

# Hospice Design Manual

## Service Area

The service entrance will open onto a service yard. (see Entrances, Section 2, page 25)

This area should be screened from view and contain enough area to allow all delivery vehicles room to maneuver.

These will include:
- Food delivery vehicles
- Dumpster collectors
- Laundry vans
- Oxygen delivery vans (if bottles are to be used)
- Equipment and furniture delivery trucks

With larger hospices, a raised dock should be considered. In all hospices the service entrance will have to allow delivered items to be wheeled into the building.

A covered unloading area is desirable.

The service area will need space to house a variety of dumpsters including:
- Biohazard waste
- General waste
- Recyclable waste

Regulations may require the Biohazard waste to be stored in a secure enclosure.

If bottled, piped-in oxygen is to be used, space must be allocated for the storage of empty tanks, and a covered manifold area provided for the full tanks.

If portable oxygen tanks are to be used, they require two separate storage areas, full and empty.

In both cases full tanks will have to be stored in a secure enclosure, which should be covered in areas which receive snow.

The service yard should not be used by funeral directors to collect deceased patients, because an accompanying family member would have an unpleasant experience seeing the body, of a loved one being loaded into the funeral director's vehicle next to several dumpsters.

Oxygen storage and used linen storage are amongst the two most flammable areas in a hospice. The service entrance will most likely also be a fire exit, so care should be taken not to place these storage areas immediately next to the service entrance.

Certain staff members (such as maintenance staff) may wish to enter the building through the service entrance and should be provided with adequate parking.

The site layout should ensure that it is clear to arriving vehicles where to go – especially with large delivery vehicles, which may have drivers who have not made deliveries to the hospice before.

The site layout should also allow plenty of room for large vehicles to maneuver, and to allow for efficient snow removal.

### Ice machine

An ice machine should be available to provide shaved ice, which can be gently dripped into a patient's mouth when they have difficulty drinking.

Ideally it will be located where both nursing staff and family members can access it – such as the patient area snack bar.

### Hazardous drug handling system.

Since anticancer and certain other drugs can be genotoxic and can cause birth defects, miscarriage, and even cancer, a safe system for handling hazardous drugs should be put in place to protect nursing staff.

'PhaSeal' is such a system. It is a closed system designed to assist with hazardous drug handling. 'PhaSeal' products use a double membrane to ensure leak-free transfers.

With this system the hazardous drugs have no contact with the atmosphere, since all connections are dry, thus protecting workers from exposure. It also features pressure equalization, preventing vapor leakage.

### Hoists

Several hoists may be used in the hospice. These can be portable and used for such applications as transferring a patient from a wheelchair to a bathtub, or they can be permanently installed to transfer a patient from their bed into the bathroom or from a gurney into the bed.

Permanently installed hoists need to be carefully located in the design to ensure that they are appropriately placed and the structure can take the weight of the hoist and patient.

Adequate storage space is required for portable hoists.

### Recumbent Bathing Systems

A bathtub such as those offered by Arjo, Noram Solutions, Vancare, Invacare and Penner patient care, will be required for the specially equipped bathroom. These allow patients to enjoy the therapeutic benefits of bathing in a safe and comfortable manner.

Several of these tubs allow nurses to raise or lower the bathing tub to provide an optimum work height while assisting the patient. They also have such options available as; hydro-massage, hydro-sound (a system for cleaning sensitive skin), auto-fill, and a built-in disinfection system. Other features include touch pad digital temperature and mixing control panels.

These companies also provide systems for transporting patients from their beds to the bathtub in comfort, enabling a single caregiver to make the transfer with a minimum of effort.

*(see Section 6, Links to Suppliers, page 139)*

# Hospice Design Manual

## Use of Color

The use of color inside a hospice building is an important tool in creating the desired atmosphere.

This includes carpet and other flooring colors, wall colors, and colors of accessories and furnishings.

Correct use of color can create more productive work spaces for the staff, and can create more relaxing rooms for the patients and their family members. Color has the ability to alter people's moods and affect the way they feel, and can lead to feelings of warmth, intimacy, and serenity, or colors can excite and stimulate.

Studies show that, for example, purple can stimulate imagination, orange can stimulate aggression, red can increase energy and appetite whilst blue can decrease heart rate. Most colors cause mixed reactions some good some bad. Blue for example can be calming and can decrease heart rate but can also cause depression – hence 'the blues'.

To avoid strong reactions from any color their use should be minimized and be subtle.

Volumes have been written on the use of color and detailed reference on the subject is recommended, together with the use of an interior designer.

But briefly, colors fall generally into two groups – warm and cool. Warm colors are the ones to be used in a hospice – we have all experienced the cold gray or green of hospital walls.

The color itself though doesn't define whether it's warm or cool. It is defined by the combination of the color and the light falling on it.

For example, a gray corridor illuminated by fluorescent lights will be in the gray/green range and will feel cool. A gray corridor with windows and with sunlight streaming in will be in the yellow/red/grey range and will feel warm.

Use of natural light where possible is therefore a high priority, as is the selection of artificial lighting. For full effect the color scheme should be coordinated with the lighting scheme to ensure compatibility. Use of a spectrometer establishes the quality of light in a given place.

Any color which combined with light falls into the red/yellow range should work well. Green is the one color whose full range of attributes seem be beneficial to a hospice situation – it is considered restful, pain soothing, and can be uplifting. Greens in the warm range would therefore be a suitable choice.

Natural wood is very warm and can be used liberally – window sills, furniture, doors etc.

In general, warm off-whites are a good choice for patient bedroom walls. They are neutral and the color can be picked up in the curtains and fabrics. Warm green carpeting or natural wood laminate flooring are good choices for flooring.

## Water Features

Incorporating water features into the architecture of a hospice is very appropriate.

Water features have a relaxing effect, can help add tranquility to spaces, and can refresh the air around them.

They can be installed inside or outside.

- Interior applications are generally quite small and focus on the sound of trickling water.

- Exterior ones can have more of a visual impact, such as fountains, waterfalls and ponds. In a courtyard or close to the building the sound also plays an important roll.

It is possible to bring a pond into the building as done in Mt. Edgecumbe Hospice, UK, by bringing glass down into the pond a few inches, creating a barrier for airflow but allowing water to circulate underneath. Any ponds should be shallow for safety reasons.

Exterior water features which utilize pump-driven flowing water are unsuitable for any part of the country which experiences any amount of frost.

If a retention pond is required in the site layout, advantage should be taken to use it to help create a beautiful vista, rather than the more typical mud hole.

# HOSPICE DESIGN MANUAL

## Works of Art

The presence of works of art in and around a hospice can add a relaxing, contemplative atmosphere with careful selection and display.

A small percentage of the cost of each project could be designated to purchase selected artwork.

Unlike in Europe, too little is generally spent on the addition of works of art to architectural projects in the USA. The benefits of having artwork to look at are substantial, especially in such a building as a hospice, and should be considered carefully.

Local artists should be encouraged to place their works on temporary display.

Two forms to be considered:

- Exterior
- Interior

### Exterior

Outdoor sculptures and water features can provide focal points and complement views in the hospice grounds and can define seating areas and other outdoor spaces.

Courtyards in the building are especially suitable for sculpture and help in the goal of creating contemplative space.

Exterior artwork is usually commissioned specifically for a particular project and can provide exposure and work for local artists.

### Interior

The presence of artwork within a hospice is another tool at our disposal for helping to create a 'non-institutional' feel to the building.

Interior artwork can be in the form of paintings, prints, woven wall hangings, sculptures, water features, etc.

Nooks can be designed into the floor plan to provide sculpture display areas.

Hospices are complex buildings with many different people using them in a variety of ways.

The following flowcharts have been developed in an attempt to identify all the different users and their individual movement through a hospice building.

1. Patient Flowchart:
   - A. Symptom Control and Respite Care
   - B. Terminal Care
   - C. Day Patient Care
   - D. Residential Care

2. Guest Flowchart:
   - A. Relatives/friends visiting patients
   - B. Relatives/friends visiting bereavement suite
   - C. Relatives/friends visiting deceased patient in room
   - D. Relatives/friends/volunteers bringing/collecting day care patients

3. Nursing Staff Flowchart

4. Administrative Staff Flowchart

5. Doctors, Therapists, Special Caregivers Flowchart

6. Volunteer Staff Flowchart

7. Custodial Staff Flowchart

8. Maintenance Staff Flowchart

9. Kitchen Staff Flowchart

10. Supplies and Waste Flowchart:
    - A. Incoming supplies
    - B. Outgoing waste / returns

11. Laundry Flowchart
    - A. In-house
    - B. Contracted

12. Deceased Patients Flowchart

13. Funeral Director Flowchart

14. Conference / Seminar Participant Flowchart

15. Home Hospice Staff Flowchart

# HOSPICE DESIGN MANUAL

## Patient Flowchart A

### Patients receiving Symptom Control and Respite Care

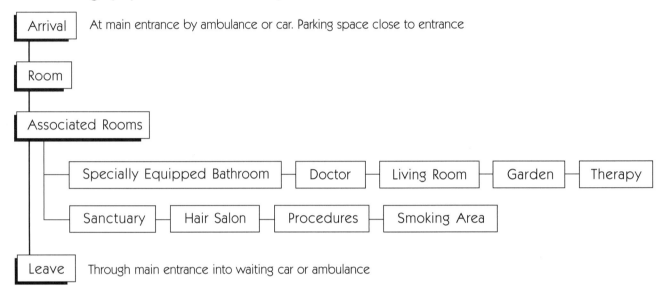

**Arrival** — At main entrance by ambulance or car. Parking space close to entrance

**Room**

**Associated Rooms**

- Specially Equipped Bathroom — Doctor — Living Room — Garden — Therapy
- Sanctuary — Hair Salon — Procedures — Smoking Area

**Leave** — Through main entrance into waiting car or ambulance

**Patients Receiving Terminal Care**

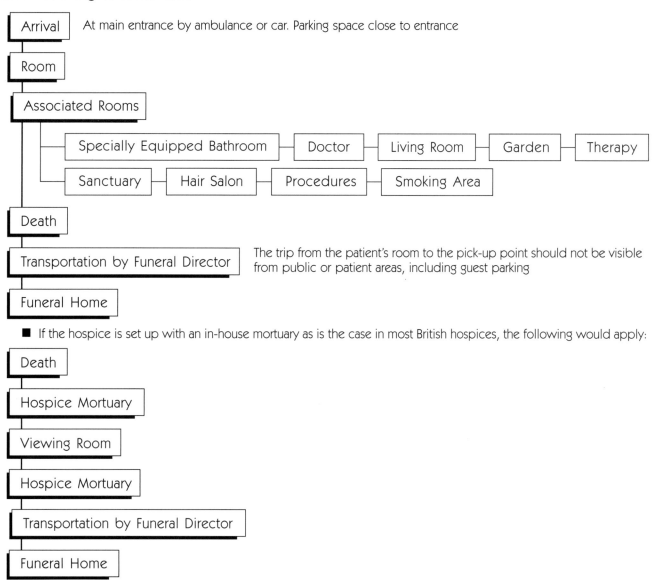

Arrival — At main entrance by ambulance or car. Parking space close to entrance

Room

Associated Rooms

Specially Equipped Bathroom — Doctor — Living Room — Garden — Therapy

Sanctuary — Hair Salon — Procedures — Smoking Area

Death

Transportation by Funeral Director — The trip from the patient's room to the pick-up point should not be visible from public or patient areas, including guest parking

Funeral Home

■ If the hospice is set up with an in-house mortuary as is the case in most British hospices, the following would apply:

Death

Hospice Mortuary

Viewing Room

Hospice Mortuary

Transportation by Funeral Director

Funeral Home

# HOSPICE DESIGN MANUAL

## Patient Flowchart C

### Patients Attending Day Care Center

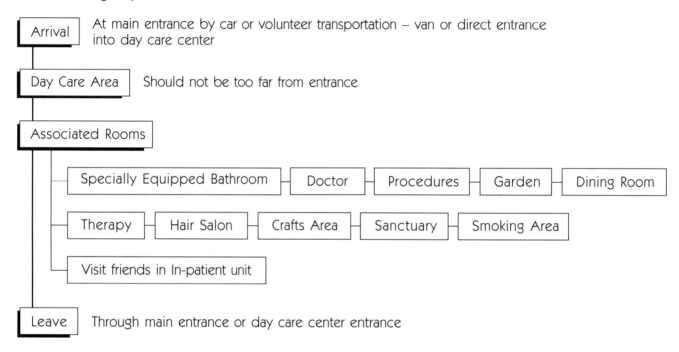

**Arrival** — At main entrance by car or volunteer transportation – van or direct entrance into day care center

**Day Care Area** — Should not be too far from entrance

**Associated Rooms**

Specially Equipped Bathroom — Doctor — Procedures — Garden — Dining Room

Therapy — Hair Salon — Crafts Area — Sanctuary — Smoking Area

Visit friends in In-patient unit

**Leave** — Through main entrance or day care center entrance

**Patients Receiving Residential Care**

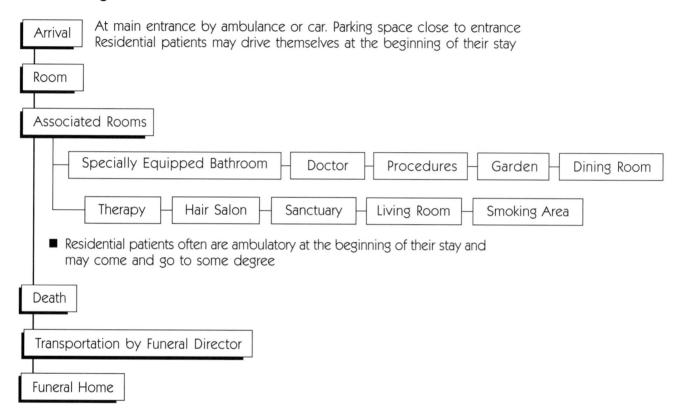

Arrival — At main entrance by ambulance or car. Parking space close to entrance
Residential patients may drive themselves at the beginning of their stay

Room

Associated Rooms

Specially Equipped Bathroom — Doctor — Procedures — Garden — Dining Room

Therapy — Hair Salon — Sanctuary — Living Room — Smoking Area

- Residential patients often are ambulatory at the beginning of their stay and may come and go to some degree

Death

Transportation by Funeral Director

Funeral Home

- See page 51 for hospices with an in-house mortuary

# HOSPICE DESIGN MANUAL

## Guest Flowchart A

### Relatives and Friends Visiting Patients

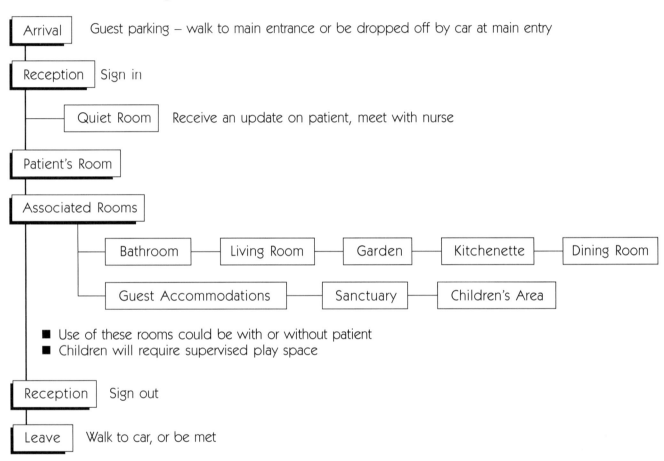

Arrival — Guest parking — walk to main entrance or be dropped off by car at main entry

Reception — Sign in

Quiet Room — Receive an update on patient, meet with nurse

Patient's Room

Associated Rooms

Bathroom — Living Room — Garden — Kitchenette — Dining Room

Guest Accommodations — Sanctuary — Children's Area

- Use of these rooms could be with or without patient
- Children will require supervised play space

Reception — Sign out

Leave — Walk to car, or be met

**Relatives and Friends Visiting Bereavement Suite (if provided)**

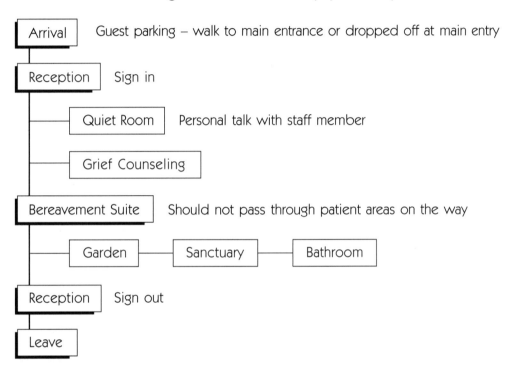

Arrival — Guest parking – walk to main entrance or dropped off at main entry

Reception — Sign in

Quiet Room — Personal talk with staff member

Grief Counseling

Bereavement Suite — Should not pass through patient areas on the way

Garden — Sanctuary — Bathroom

Reception — Sign out

Leave

# HOSPICE DESIGN MANUAL

## Guest Flowchart C

**Relatives and Friends Visiting Deceased Patient in Room**

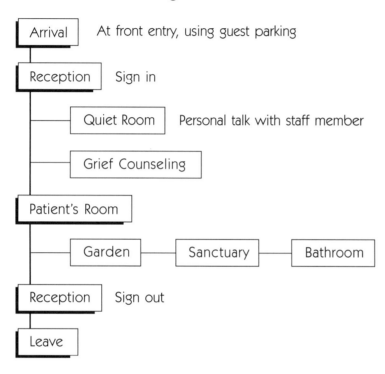

Arrival — At front entry, using guest parking

Reception — Sign in

Quiet Room — Personal talk with staff member

Grief Counseling

Patient's Room

Garden — Sanctuary — Bathroom

Reception — Sign out

Leave

**Relatives / Social Workers / Friends / Volunteers Bringing and Collecting Day Care Center Patients**

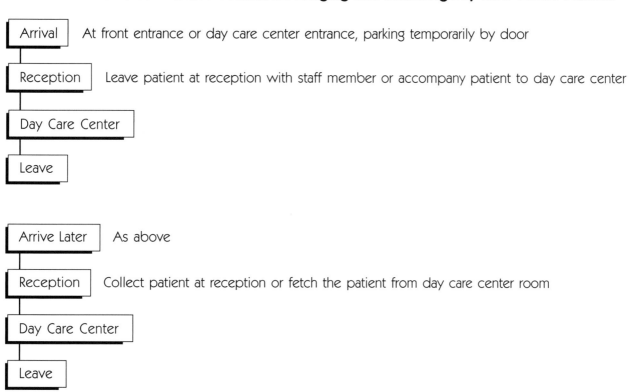

| Arrival | At front entrance or day care center entrance, parking temporarily by door |

| Reception | Leave patient at reception with staff member or accompany patient to day care center |

Day Care Center

Leave

| Arrive Later | As above |

| Reception | Collect patient at reception or fetch the patient from day care center room |

Day Care Center

Leave

# HOSPICE DESIGN MANUAL

## Nursing Staff Flowchart

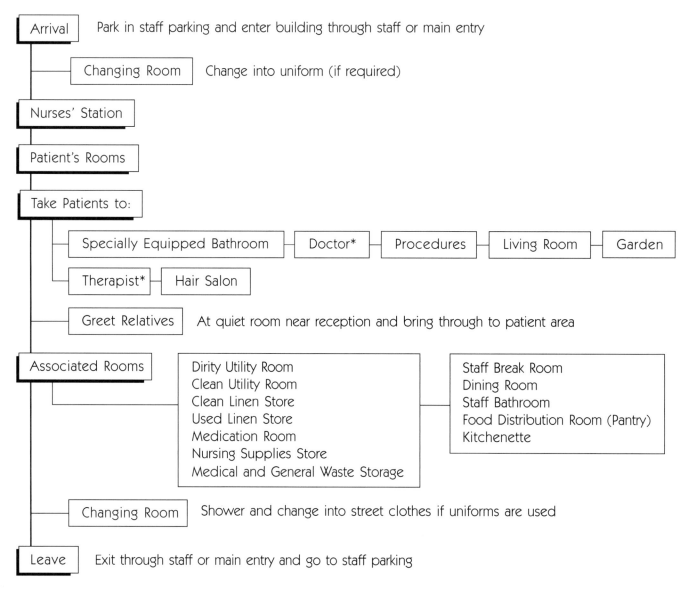

Arrival — Park in staff parking and enter building through staff or main entry

Changing Room — Change into uniform (if required)

Nurses' Station

Patient's Rooms

Take Patients to:

Specially Equipped Bathroom — Doctor* — Procedures — Living Room — Garden

Therapist* — Hair Salon

Greet Relatives — At quiet room near reception and bring through to patient area

Associated Rooms

Dirity Utility Room
Clean Utility Room
Clean Linen Store
Used Linen Store
Medication Room
Nursing Supplies Store
Medical and General Waste Storage

Staff Break Room
Dining Room
Staff Bathroom
Food Distribution Room (Pantry)
Kitchenette

Changing Room — Shower and change into street clothes if uniforms are used

Leave — Exit through staff or main entry and go to staff parking

*In many cases doctors and therapists will go to the patient's room

## Administrative Staff Flowchart

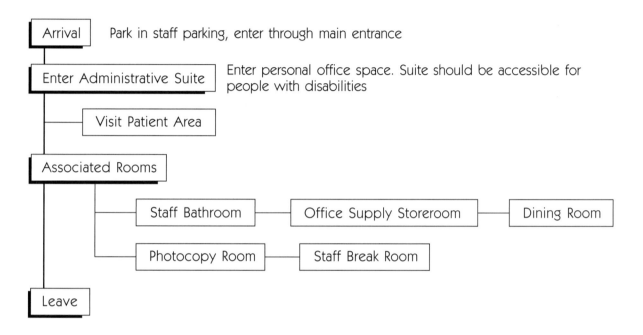

Arrival — Park in staff parking, enter through main entrance

Enter Administrative Suite — Enter personal office space. Suite should be accessible for people with disabilities

Visit Patient Area

Associated Rooms

Staff Bathroom — Office Supply Storeroom — Dining Room

Photocopy Room — Staff Break Room

Leave

# HOSPICE DESIGN MANUAL

## Doctors, Therapists, Special Caregivers Flowchart

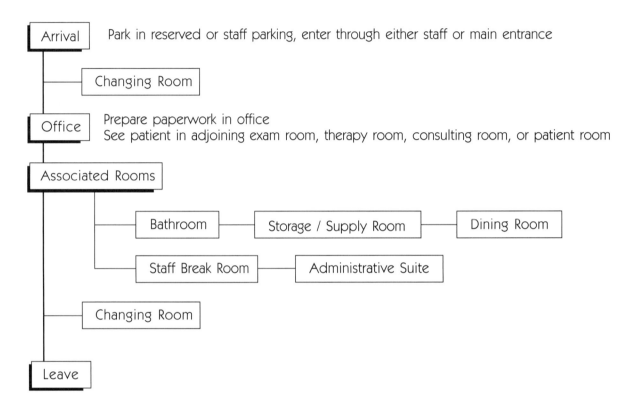

**Arrival** — Park in reserved or staff parking, enter through either staff or main entrance

Changing Room

**Office** — Prepare paperwork in office
See patient in adjoining exam room, therapy room, consulting room, or patient room

**Associated Rooms**

Bathroom — Storage / Supply Room — Dining Room

Staff Break Room — Administrative Suite

Changing Room

**Leave**

## Volunteer Staff Flowchart

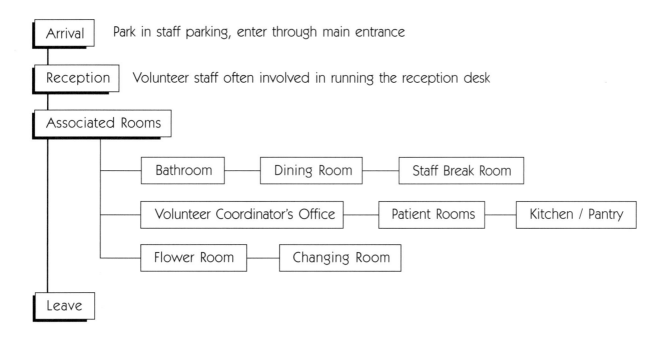

| Arrival | Park in staff parking, enter through main entrance |

| Reception | Volunteer staff often involved in running the reception desk |

Associated Rooms

Bathroom — Dining Room — Staff Break Room

Volunteer Coordinator's Office — Patient Rooms — Kitchen / Pantry

Flower Room — Changing Room

Leave

■ This flowchart will depend on each volunteer's specific assignments in the hospice

# HOSPICE DESIGN MANUAL

## Custodial Staff Flowchart

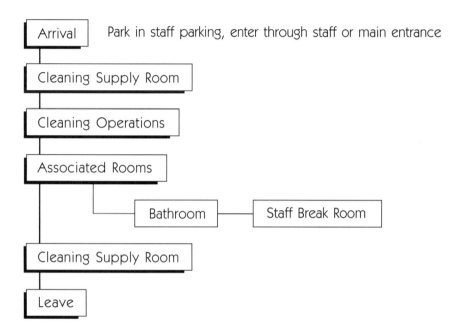

Arrival — Park in staff parking, enter through staff or main entrance

Cleaning Supply Room

Cleaning Operations

Associated Rooms

Bathroom — Staff Break Room

Cleaning Supply Room

Leave

## Maintenance Staff Flowchart

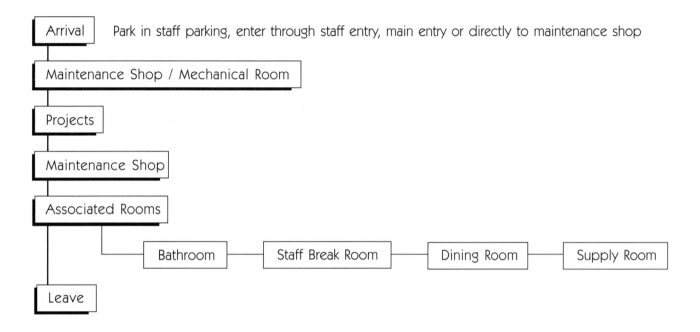

Arrival — Park in staff parking, enter through staff entry, main entry or directly to maintenance shop

Maintenance Shop / Mechanical Room

Projects

Maintenance Shop

Associated Rooms

Bathroom — Staff Break Room — Dining Room — Supply Room

Leave

# Hospice Design Manual

## Kitchen Staff Flowchart

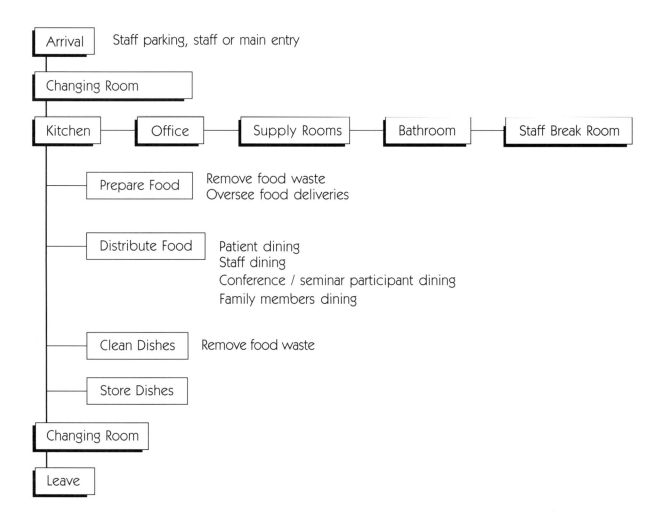

Arrival — Staff parking, staff or main entry

Changing Room

Kitchen — Office — Supply Rooms — Bathroom — Staff Break Room

Prepare Food — Remove food waste / Oversee food deliveries

Distribute Food — Patient dining / Staff dining / Conference / seminar participant dining / Family members dining

Clean Dishes — Remove food waste

Store Dishes

Changing Room

Leave

## A. Incoming Supplies

| | |
|---|---|
| Food Supplies | Kitchen, dry storage, frozen, refrigerated, produce |
| Nursing Supplies | Secure items, drugs, to medication room, non-secure items to nursing supply store |
| Office Supplies | To administrative-area store |
| Cleaning Supplies | To cleaning room (secure storage for hazardous cleaning materials) |
| Clean Linen | To clean linen store (if contracted) |
| Oxygen Bottles | To Oxygen store |
| Maintenance Items | To maintenance store |

## B. Outgoing Waste / Returns

| | |
|---|---|
| Food Waste | From kitchen |
| Biohazardous Medical Waste | Secure dry storage |
| Recyclables | Paper, bottles, cans, etc., from entire facility |
| General Trash | From entire facility |
| Empty Oxygen Bottles | From patient area |
| Dirty Laundry | If contracted, from patient area |

## Laundry Flowchart

### A. In-house Laundry

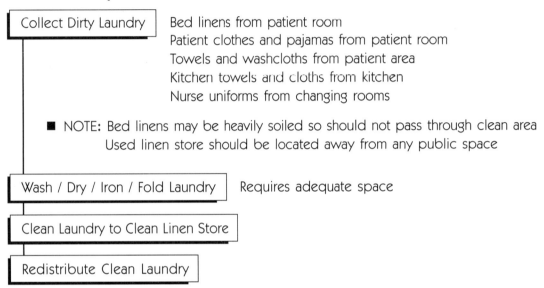

| Collect Dirty Laundry | Bed linens from patient room |
|---|---|

Patient clothes and pajamas from patient room
Towels and washcloths from patient area
Kitchen towels and cloths from kitchen
Nurse uniforms from changing rooms

■ NOTE: Bed linens may be heavily soiled so should not pass through clean area
Used linen store should be located away from any public space

| Wash / Dry / Iron / Fold Laundry | Requires adequate space |
|---|---|

Clean Laundry to Clean Linen Store

Redistribute Clean Laundry

### B. Contracted Laundry Service

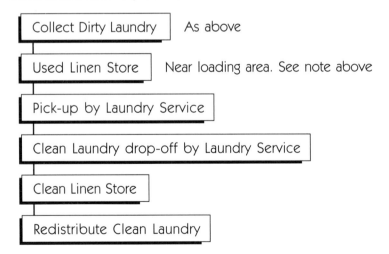

| Collect Dirty Laundry | As above |
|---|---|

| Used Linen Store | Near loading area. See note above |
|---|---|

Pick-up by Laundry Service

Clean Laundry drop-off by Laundry Service

Clean Linen Store

Redistribute Clean Laundry

## Deceased Patient's Flowchart

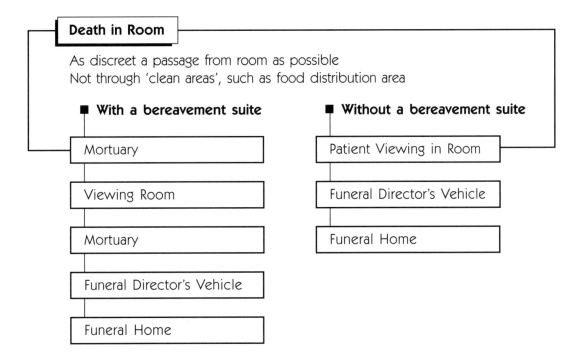

**Death in Room**

As discreet a passage from room as possible
Not through 'clean areas', such as food distribution area

■ **With a bereavement suite**

Mortuary

Viewing Room

Mortuary

Funeral Director's Vehicle

Funeral Home

■ **Without a bereavement suite**

Patient Viewing in Room

Funeral Director's Vehicle

Funeral Home

# Hospice Design Manual

## Funeral Director Flowchart

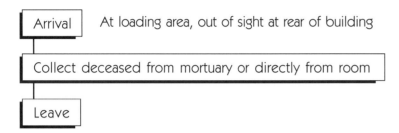

Arrival — At loading area, out of sight at rear of building

Collect deceased from mortuary or directly from room

Leave

- Site layout should ensure that the funeral director's vehicle is not driven directly past main entry, or through guest parking area, and is not visible from patient rooms

- An attached garage could be used for the most discreet collection

- Use of a hearse is to be strongly discouraged, plain vans or station wagons being the preferred vehicles

## Conference / Seminar Participant Flowchart

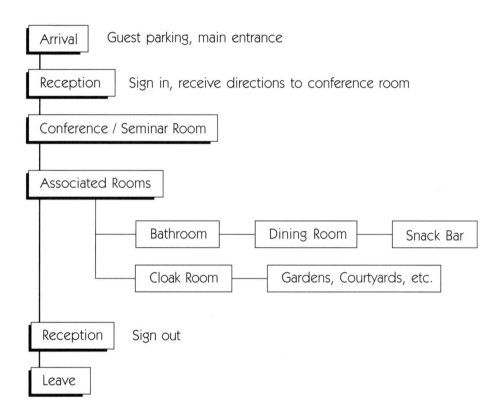

Arrival — Guest parking, main entrance

Reception — Sign in, receive directions to conference room

Conference / Seminar Room

Associated Rooms

Bathroom — Dining Room — Snack Bar

Cloak Room — Gardens, Courtyards, etc.

Reception — Sign out

Leave

# HOSPICE DESIGN MANUAL

## Home Hospice Staff Flowchart

**A.M.**

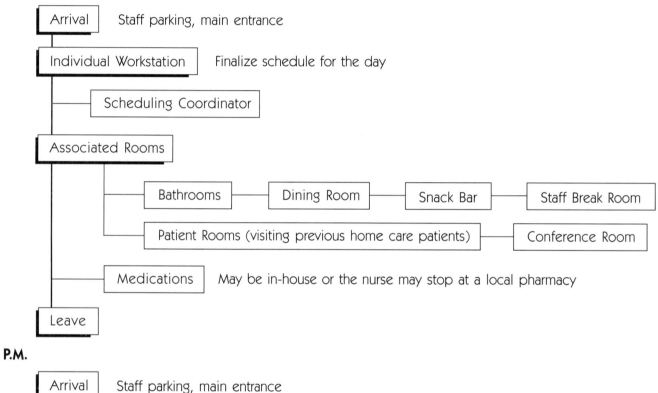

Arrival — Staff parking, main entrance

Individual Workstation — Finalize schedule for the day

Scheduling Coordinator

Associated Rooms

Bathrooms → Dining Room → Snack Bar → Staff Break Room

Patient Rooms (visiting previous home care patients) → Conference Room

Medications — May be in-house or the nurse may stop at a local pharmacy

Leave

**P.M.**

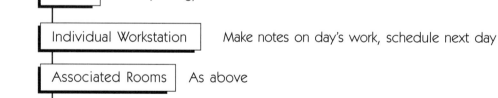

Arrival — Staff parking, main entrance

Individual Workstation — Make notes on day's work, schedule next day

Associated Rooms — As above

Scheduling Coordinator

Leave

## Section 4 – Individual Room Notes

**Patient Area**
Patient Room
Nurses' Station
Living Room
Medication Room
Quiet Rooms
Smoking Room / Area
Family Accommodations
Pharmacy
Pantry
Dirty Utility Room
Clean Utility Room
Physical Therapy Room
Hair Salon
Specially Equipped Bathroom
Snack Bar
Computer Room and Computers
Treatment and Exam Rooms
Multi-sensory Room
Complementary Therapy Rooms

**Public Area**
Reception
Sanctuary
Dining Room
Library
Consulting Rooms
Body Removal / Bereavement Suite
Bathrooms
Shop

**Service Area**
Kitchen
Flower Room
Used Linen Room
Clean Linen Room
Laundry Facilities
Storage
Changing / Locker Rooms
Staff Break Room
Mechanical / Communications / Electrical Rooms
Custodians' Room and Cleaning Closets
Oxygen Room

**Administration Area**
Offices
Home Hospice Department

**Education**
Classrooms
Conference Rooms

**Day Care Center**

*Some room notes contain information relative to other areas*

# Hospice Design Manual

## Room Notes – Patient Area

### PATIENT ROOM

The patient rooms are the primary space in any hospice.

In reality many if not most in-patients will only see their rooms. They won't see the exterior of the hospice if they arrive by ambulance, and if bed bound, won't see the other areas within the hospice. The patient rooms need to be as comfortable as possible for the patients, whilst enabling the staff to carry out their tasks and allowing family members to visit without crowding.

Whilst multiple beds in a room decrease the required square footage per bed, and the number of bathrooms required, they also immediately destroy any attempt to create a homelike atmosphere. They lack the privacy required to preserve a patient's dignity, and lack the privacy required for the patient's loved ones to say their private farewells. For these reasons single rooms with a private bath are recommended.

The patient room can be split into four different areas:
- Patient bed area
- Patient bathroom
- Patio or Balcony
- Family area

### Patient Bed Area
- Should have adequate space on both sides of the bed to allow unobstructed access by staff and to assist the patient with hoists if necessary

- Requires a headwall system of some kind (*see below*)
- Should have soft lighting with the potential for brighter light for examinations
- Avoid lights shining in the patient's eyes
- Should be provided with an oxygen supply of some kind (*see Oxygen Supply, Section 2, page 37*)
- Should have an effective call system (*see Call Systems, Section 2, page 39*)
- Consider the possibility of a ceiling-mounted hoist system (could also be connected to the bathroom)
- Allow for a direct line of vision of the patient from the door. This allows nurses to just crack the door and check that the patient is all right without disturbing the patient or family
- Electric beds allow the patient to select different positions. Heights can be adjusted for examinations. (Several companies have large selections of electric beds and other patient room furniture.)
- Should have a telephone with the option of turning the ringer off

Generally there is a console known as a headwall system at the bed head containing power outlets, a call system, oxygen and vacuum (if supplied), and lighting. The consoles tend to give a clinical presence

**PATIENT ROOM** *(Continued)*

to the room. Sliding picture units are available as one of several choices to conceal the console while it is not in use.

The Hill-Rom Company for example offers several headwall systems suitable for a hospice, which incorporate different combinations of suction, air, oxygen, individual A/C and heat controls, aromatherapy units, notice boards, and different levels of lighting in a variety of styles.

### Patient Bathroom

Some patients will be unable to use the bathroom and will have to use bedpans and be given bed baths. However allowing patients to have full use of the bathroom gives them more dignity. The bathroom should therefore be designed to allow nursing staff or caregivers to assist the patient while they use the bathroom.

It is best not to place the toilet in the standard corner location (which works well with an unassisted patient) but to locate it along a wall where it can be accessed on each side. If a patient collapses on the toilet in a corner setup it is exceedingly difficult to get around and lift the patient especially if they are heavy.

Drop-down hand rails on each side of the toilet are required to provide the accessibility when the toilet is not located in the corner. Neaco is one company providing such rails *(see Section 6, Links to Suppliers, page 139)*

Many patients are unable to use a shower. So, whilst convenient a shower is not an absolute necessity in all patient rooms. Patients able to use a shower could perhaps go a short distance to a separate shower room.

However, if the room may also be used for residential care a shower is necessary, as these patients tend to be more ambulatory.

The entire bathroom can be carefully designed to function as a shower room with a central drain, with the shower head pointed away from the sink and toilet. This alleviates the need for a separate shower stall which in reality may seldom get used.

There are several different designs of shower door and curtains available. The goal is to keep the nurses from getting soaked whilst assisting the patient. A half-door seems to be the best solution allowing a nurse to lean over to assist yet be away from the splashes.

Facilities are needed to empty bed pans and bedside commodes. Traditionally these were taken to a 'sluice room' to be flushed out and then sterilized, but by providing a spray attachment to the toilet they can be emptied in the bathroom toilet and then carried empty to be sterilized, alleviating the unpleasant job of transporting a full bedpan.

The bathroom needs a towel rack, storage for towels, wash cloths and soap, a paper towel dispenser, a lined trash receptacle, and a hand sanitizer.

## Room Notes – Patient Area *(continued)*

### Family Area

There should be space within the room to allow family members and friends to visit.

A table and chairs provides a place for children to occupy themselves during a visit helping everyone to relax.

A reclining chair should be provided so a relative may spend the night. It may also be used by the patient.

Providing accommodations in the patient room for family members to spend the night gives the impression that it is expected. Both patients and family members require their privacy and long visits can be exhausting to both. Separate sleeping accommodations close by provide the necessary privacy but allow the family members to be right there when they need to be. *(see Family Accommodations, Section 4, page 79)*

### Patio or Balcony

Ideally all patient rooms should open onto a balcony or patio.

- If possible, provide a covered area
- Have a threshold which is easy to wheel a bed or wheelchair over.
- An outdoor electrical outlet allows an electric bed to be plugged in.
- May need to have insect screens.
- These can be private or shared. Shared outdoor areas allow family members to interact with different families.

### Room Size

Specific local and state regulations may require a minimum patient room size, but rooms between 250 and 300 square feet work the best. (Not including the bathroom.)

Consideration may be given to provide one larger bedroom where a couple could be together if they both required hospice care. This would require two sets of headwall consoles. However terminally ill partners sharing a room can cause unexpected problems for staff, as they tend to worry more about each other than their own well-being.

### In general the room needs:

- Storage space for some of the patients' clothes and belongings
- A card-display area in view of the patient
- Lots of shelving
- A flower display area
- A pleasant view with low windowsills allowing a patient to see out from the bed
- Sunlight at some point in the day with an overhang to prevent glare
- Sufficient number of electrical outlets at waist height
- Doors wide enough to wheel a bed through, minimum of 3-feet 8-inches
- Screened windows

## Room Notes – Patient Area *(continued)*

- A television or digital entertainment system
- Computer and internet ports (these will become increasingly needed as the baby boom generation begins to age) Consider WiFi
- Possibility of a window in the door or corridor wall with adjustable curtains/blinds to allow the patient to control their degree of privacy
- Either a hand sink for nursing staff or a hand sanitizer dispenser
- Temperature controls which allow the room temperature to be set between 65°F and 80°F

### NURSES' STATION

The nurses' station is the heart and the hub of any hospice patient area.

Comfort and attention paid to this area will reflect directly on the quality of patient care. Happy nurses make happy patients.

At night the nurses' station is often the only area in a hospice with staff.

There needs to be a night entrance with good security, i.e., no place for someone to hide, brightly lit and offering good visibility for a nurse opening the door. If the main entrance is to be used at night, it should be close to patient area and should also have no concealed area.

Both the main entrance and the night entrance should have closed-circuit television cameras (CCTV) allowing nurses to monitor both entrances.

Nurses should also be able to open the door with remote lock activation. (buzzer system)

The central security alarm control panel should be located in the nurses' station.

If there is a separate ambulance entry directly into the patient area for arriving patients – this could be utilized as a night entry.

Nurses, due the job they do, need to let off steam, and often do this through laughter. Some relatives might find this inappropriate so privacy in the nurses' station is essential.

The staff break room and charting area away from the main desk are more appropriate places for 'letting-off steam.'

#### Requirements:

- Private charting area to write up reports, etc.
- Desk with phone, fax, CCTV, computer, call system, and alarm system
- Several phones for use during peak moments
- Emergency flashlights, small supplemental fire extinguishers

#### Related areas:

- Medication room
- Nursing and medical supply rooms
- Locker room with shower
- Staff break room
- Nurses' bathroom

# HOSPICE DESIGN MANUAL

## Room Notes – Patient Area *(continued)*

### NURSES' STATION *(Continued)*

- Doctors' office – good communication with doctor is essential
- Bedpan sterilizing room (with sluice if used)
- Small laundry

### There are two schools of thought:

- Nurses' station should be plainly visible with counter, hospital-style.
- Nurses' Station should be discreetly off to the side of the patient area with just a door leading to it – often a Dutch door.

In either case there needs to be a confidential area which cannot be accessed by visitors. Otherwise, nurses need to close down computer screens, cover up writing and stop discussing patients, per HIPAA requirements.

If relatives are allowed to access patients' rooms via patio doors the security alarm system requires individual room controls on the system panel.

The nurses' station should be placed as central to all rooms as possible, with no long, daunting corridors to minimize travel distances for nurses. *(North Carolina regulations call for a maximum travel distance of 150 feet from the nurse's station to furthest patient room.)*

Allow extra space for volunteers to sit near the nurses' station to assist relatives and visitors.

Also required in or near this area is a private office for the nurse manager – where the nurse manager may hold confidential conversations with nursing staff.

### LIVING ROOM

The living room is a comfortable, cozy space located near the patient area. Usually equipped with comfortable chairs and couches, bookshelves, a television, a stereo system, and a space for small children to play with toys.

It is used primarily by visiting family members to relax, mingle with other families, and share experiences. Ambulatory patients will also use the space to visit with their family or just to sit somewhere different, so space should be allotted to accommodate wheelchairs.

The room should have a sunny aspect and ideally will have patio doors leading to the hospice garden.

The room should be located close to the patient area to encourage its use, but should not be adjacent to the nurses' station as this is the busiest area of the hospice.

Depending on the size of the hospice, multiple living rooms are a possibility, with two or more smaller rooms close to the patient areas rather than a large central room.

Fireplaces create an intimate atmosphere, but if used should be gas-fired for safety and compliance with local fire regulations.

## Room Notes – Patient Area *(continued)*

### MEDICATION ROOM

This room is for storage and preparation of medications.

- Nurses spend a good deal of time working in the room so it should be provided with natural light.

- Windows and doors need to be secure.

- Storage for scheduled drugs requires locking as per regulations, and storage space needs to be provided for non-scheduled drugs.

- Requires a sink, a regular and a locked refrigerator and adequate counter space. *(see note page 81)*

- Needs space for two nurses to work at the same time.

- Needs space for trolley storage and space for trolley in work area (if a trolley system is utilized).

- Needs convenient location to the nurses' station – entrance to the room should be observed by nurses, ideally accessible only from the nurses' station.

Narcotics storage needs to be provided in accordance with any federal, state, and other applicable laws. Typically a double-locked cabinet at eye level is required for non-perishable drugs, and a double-locked 'drugs only' refrigerator provided for those requiring refrigeration. The refrigerator would need to maintain a temperature range between 36°F and 46°F.

Some anticancer drugs are genotoxic and can cause birth defects, miscarriage and even cancer. These drugs require 'safe handling' and a system such as 'PhaSeal' should be considered to assist with hazardous drug handling (Supplied by Baxa Corporation).

*(see Specialized Equipment, Section 2, page 45)*

# HOSPICE DESIGN MANUAL

## Room Notes – Patient Area *(continued)*

### QUIET ROOMS

Quiet rooms are small rooms which provide privacy to family members, a place to go and have a 'good cry', or one in which a staff member may have a conversation with a family member – either for an update or to break bad news.

Ideally one should be located near the main entry. This should be larger as it may be used by a staff member to meet with a family as soon as they arrive to discuss the current situation.

One should be equipped with a telephone to allow relatives a private space to break the news of a death to others.

In the patient area quiet rooms should also be available as a place for a relative to 'get away' for a while.

After a patient dies, the family may be asked to stay in a quiet room while the patient is cleaned up and the bed linen changed. They then may return to the patient's room and pay their last respects.

The quiet rooms should have natural light and comfortable furnishings and be soundproofed to ensure the privacy of those within.

Quiet rooms may also double up for use by counselors, and should have a sign outside indicating if the room is in use.

### SMOKING ROOM / AREA

Some hospices provide a designated smoking room inside the building, whilst others allow smoking only outside or allow smoking in a screened porch.

A designated interior room is generally for patient use only, so I have included this area in the 'Patient area' section, but the room itself should be located far enough away from the patient area to ensure that no smoke smell reaches the patient rooms.

Location of designated smoking room:
- Away from patient rooms, as smell travels
- In a position where nurses can observe occupants (in case they fall asleep)
- Convenient to both day-care and in-patients

Requirements:
- Should have a hard surface floor – not carpet to avoid burns and smell retention, and have fire retardant upholstery
- Should have blinds in place of curtains
- Needs a good ventilation system, separate from the rest of the building, and windows that open
- Should have an exterior door to encourage smoking outside, but security needs to be taken into account.

If patient rooms have patios on which they may smoke, the patio should not be shared with another room.

If a screened area is provided for smoking, another one should be provided for non-smokers since screens and the furniture take on the smell of smoke.

### FAMILY ACCOMMODATIONS

Separate accommodations should be provided to allow family members to sleep in the hospice building separately from the patient but be near their loved one.

Patients require peace and quiet at certain times and there should be a place to where relatives can 'disappear'.

Relatives need to be able to visit as necessary but also need quiet time away. *(see Patient Rooms, Section 4, page 74)*

Family accommodations can be provided as a suite, or as a designated room.

- A designated family room should have full bath facilities available for non-patients. Relatives should not use patient bathrooms to prevent cross infection.

- Family suites should accommodate up to four people, preferably with attached full bathroom.

Usually a double bed and a sleeper sofas are provided.

Family suites should be adjacent to patient areas so as not to feel isolated at night when the rest of building is shut down, and also to be close to the patient.

They should be near to a kitchenette and laundry facilities.

A typical stay in a family suite in Great Britain is for three nights.

Family suites need to be accessed by the main or the night entry, not with a private entry – for security reasons, and to allow nursing staff to keep track of who is in the building at night.

Two suites for each 16 patient beds is desirable.

Any accommodations provided should be fully accessible.

Some relatives will temporarily move into the patient's home and don't require accommodations at the hospice.

If family accommodations are too comfortable there is a danger of the family 'setting up residence', so the accommodations whilst being pleasant, need not be luxurious.

## Room Notes – Patient Area *(continued)*

### PHARMACY

Certain larger hospice facilities may decide to have an in-house pharmacist and associated pharmacy instead of the standard medication room.

For security reasons the room should be internally located or have secure windows.

The pharmacist should have an adjacent small office.

Ideally the pharmacy will have a counter (or Dutch door) opening into the nursing station.

Requirements:

- Sink area
- Refrigerator
- Counters running around the room, with adjustable shelving above, drawers and cabinets below the counter, and a central work island.
- Secure double-locking door(s) leading out of the room.

The nursing station will still need a medication cabinet and refrigerator to store medications when the pharmacy is closed, since only pharmacists or their assistants may dispense medications from the pharmacy.

### PANTRY

A pantry is generally used in a large facility or where the kitchen is a long way from the patient area.

It functions as a space where a food trolley is brought from the kitchen, food is removed from the trolley and then distributed to the patients.

The pantry may also be used for nurses to prepare and store patients' snacks.

The room needs a counter area with sink and storage cabinets, and space for the trolley to maneuver and be unloaded.

## DIRTY UTILITY ROOM

A dirty utility room contains a bedpan sanitizing unit or a sluice (bedpan flusher and sanitizer), storage space for bedpans, and a utility sink with counter.

Bedpans are hung from the wall to store.

The room is noisy when the sluice is in use and should be located in a central position near the patient area but not directly in it.

Ideally it should have a window that opens for ventilation, and an extract fan.

There should be enough space for two people to work.

Some hospices are doing without a sluice, emptying bedpans and bedside commodes into the patients' bathroom toilet. This alleviates a nurse having to carry a full bedpan from the patients' room to the dirty utility room. A spray attachment to the patient's toilet is required in this case.

If a sluice is not used, the dirty utility room would require only a bedpan sanitizer, bedpan storage space, and a utility sink and counter space.

## CLEAN UTILITY ROOM

A clean utility room should be located in the patient area with a sink, counter space, shelving and room for a linen trolley.

This is a suitable room to locate a domestic washer and dryer where family members may wash personal items or have them washed by hospice staff or volunteers. Patients' pajamas and clothes are often washed with this equipment.

NOTE: Regulations generally require that all sinks in utility rooms, medication room and exam rooms be equipped with faucets with 4-inch wrist handles.

## Room Notes – Patient Area *(continued)*

### PHYSICAL THERAPY ROOM

Physical therapy provides an important benefit to patients and can be provided in conjunction with a day care program.

A physical therapy area requires space to work with a patient, storage for several large items – exercise balls, walkers, etc., and office space for the therapist to take notes and update patient files.

Depending on the size of the program, several patients may use the space at the same time – so this should be determined early to ensure adequate space allotment.

A set of steps is a useful component in physical therapy, usually comprising of four or five steps up to a landing and the same number of steps back down, or a large enough landing to turn around to come back down.

The ceiling height in the room should be able to accommodate such steps.

The main set of stairs in the building (if two stories) can be used for this purpose, but a standard run up to a landing is too long for many patients.

The physical therapy program might initially include the use of exercise tubs, or they may be added in the future. If such tubs are not initially included, appropriate plumbing should be provided to allow for the future installation.

### HAIR SALON

A hairdressing salon can be included, especially where the hospice also offers day care and respite care.

Nothing perks up a female patient more than getting her hair done. Male patients also enjoy manicures and hair trims.

The salon itself should provide an 'uplifting' experience, and as such should itself be a pleasant room with plenty of natural light.

The ideal workstation is a free-standing chair/sink, centrally located in the room so that the hairdresser can work comfortably in front of the patient, not leaning over from the side.

Also required is a separate sink, work area, storage and room to maneuver the patient into position.

## SPECIALLY EQUIPPED BATHROOMS

Along with the bathrooms for patients included in their rooms, a separate, specially equipped bathroom should be provided.

The primary piece of equipment in this room would be a recumbent bathing system of some kind.

Tremendous relief from discomfort and stress can be achieved by utilizing such a system.

The room should be located as close to the patient rooms as possible to minimize the travel distance for patients especially if slings or hoist are used.

There are two basic systems available:

### ■ Walk-in Tub

In this system a patient steps into the tub, the door is closed, and the tub fills up with water. In older models the patients would have to sit in the tub while it drains causing them to get uncomfortably chilly. Newer models however have powered rapid draining systems which somewhat alleviate this problem.

### ■ Drop-in Tub

With these tubs patients are lowered into the tub on a padded platform or may climb in, if able. Several of the models feature adjustable heights allowing ambulatory patients to climb in at its lowest setting, and then the tub can be raised, to place it at a convenient working height for nursing staff to assist the patient.

Many tubs are equipped to provide hydromassage and other options.

Most manufacturers of recumbent bathing systems also provide an integrated transport and lifting system to lift a patient from their bed, transport them and lower them into the tub. *(see Specialized Equipment, Section 2, page 45)*

A section of the room could be 'curtained-off' allowing the room to double-up as a shower room, and should be provided with a bathing seat. A moveable shower seat is preferred to a fixed one as it allows greater flexibility and better access around the patient by nursing staff.

Also provided in the room should be a sink, and a toilet. The toilet should be equipped with drop-down handrails and allow nurses to access either side of the patient if necessary. *(see Patient Bathroom, Section 4, page 73)*

Great care should be taken with the placement of mirrors so patients cannot easily see themselves whilst unclothed. The last thing a patient near death requires is a reminder of their physical condition.

## Room Notes – Patient Area *(continued)*

### SNACK BAR

A place where visiting relatives can prepare themselves a snack at any time of night or day should be provided.

In a small hospice where the kitchen is open for anyone's use, relatives can just prepare their snacks right there, using a separate refrigerator designated for their use.

In a larger hospice and in one with a commercial kitchen, a designated snack bar should be provided. This could be located as a small room in the patient area, or in a section of the dining room and will need to be set up as a kitchenette including:

- Small refrigerator
- Counter and sink
- Microwave
- Coffee machine
- Electric kettle
- Food storage – in a way where different people's food can easily be separated
- Small table and chairs

### COMPUTER ROOM and COMPUTERS

Increasingly important is a designated computer room with one or more computers for relatives to use whilst visiting patients. The computer(s) should have Internet access, and connections should also be available for personal laptops.

The room need not be large and an alcove would suffice.

Computers should be arranged in the room to make it easy for staff and parents to supervise children using the computer, i.e. with the screen facing the door.

Patient rooms, nurses' station; treatment, therapy, and exam rooms; and all offices should also have the necessary connections available to plug a computer in and access the Internet.

Consideration should be given to installing WiFi throughout the facility, to allow laptop use anywhere.

## TREATMENT and EXAM ROOMS

It is generally nicer for patients to be examined by a doctor in their bedroom rather than in an examination room. The lighting required to perform an examination will be very different from the general lighting in the room, so specific lighting should be provided for doctors to use, with care taken not to have any bright lights shining into patients' eyes.

In a day care unit an exam room will be required and standard medical exam room requirements will apply – examination table with room for wheelchair access, counter with sink for hand washing, storage for exam gloves and other equipment, and a writing surface for the doctor with room for a laptop and the appropriate connections. Several waist high electrical outlets should be provided.

This exam room could connect directly to the doctor's office if the location was also suitably close to the patient area.

Special treatments such as those for lymphedema require a designated treatment room. This would consist of a treatment area with a counter and sink, and a large attached storeroom with adjustable shelving.

The treatment room requires space for an electric bed/couch, scales, a dressing trolley, and a desk and chair.

Patients will either walk or be wheeled into the room and be transfered to the treatment bed, requiring room to maneuver wheelchairs and hoists. A bathroom should be readily available.

A lymphedema service could extend to walk-in patients as well as in-patient and day care patients. In this case a separate entry is desirable, leading to a lymphedema suite. Lymphedema patients are often extremely self-conscious of their condition and would not want to enter the building through the main entrance. The day care entrance would be acceptable.

The lymphedema suite would comprise a reception area and small waiting room with space for informational leaflets. As well as the treatment room and storeroom as described above, the suite should have a fully accessible bathroom which includes a walk-in shower.

Lymphedema patients also use physical therapy equipment – treadmills, exercise bikes, floor mats, and a hydrotherapy pool. If such equipment is not available elsewhere in the hospice building, consideration should be given to providing space for these in the lymphedema suite. (see note page 81)

# Hospice Design Manual

## Room Notes – Patient Area *(continued)*

### MULTI-SENSORY ROOM

Most common in children's hospices, multi-sensory rooms are however present in a few adult facilities and should be given due consideration.

A multi-sensory room or 'Snoezelem' as they are known in Europe, is a room designed to stimulate the senses and to provide relaxation.

Many elderly patients and especially those with dementia suffer from sensory deprivation. Due to memory loss, deafness, and general confusion they are unable to respond to standard forms of sensory stimulation.

A multi-sensory room is a darkened room with comfortable seating and/or a water bed. Colored lights are projected onto the walls, and bubble tubes continually change color, which along with fiber-optic displays offer both visual and tactile stimulation. Olfactory stimulation is achieved with aromatherapy and auditory stimulation provided by gentle, rhythmic, hypnotic music.

The end result is an experience for the patient which is gently relaxing.

Studies have shown that sessions improve patients' anxiety levels, moods and behavior; reduce sadness and fear and increase levels of happiness and general well being. The studies also showed a change of moods for their caregivers – for the better.

Requirements for such a space are an internal room with enough space for two people to relax comfortably and room for the fiber-optic displays and bubble tubes; blank walls, four ceiling-hung projectors (one for each wall), built-in speakers and a large walk-in closet for the various equipment.

## COMPLEMENTARY THERAPY ROOMS

Several types of therapy can be offered to patients by the hospice program, and as the hospice movement develops further types of therapy can be expected.

Commonly used complementary therapy programs include:

### ■ Massage

Massage is generally performed on a massage table, massage chair, or a floor mat. Space should be allotted to store the table, chair or mat when not currently in use.

The massage therapist requires 3 feet of space all around the table in which to work. Space is required to transfer patients from a wheelchair to the work area and room to maneuver the wheelchair or portable hoist.

### ■ Aromatherapy

Aromatherapy consists of a patient relaxing to the aromas of essential oils heated up in a small portable unit. An aromatherapy room thus requires a bed with space to transfer a patient and maneuver a wheelchair and portable hoist.

It also requires a small refrigerator to store the essential oils and a seat for the therapist.

Aromatherapy may also be offered at the patient's bedside, with the equipment placed on the patient's bedside table. Some headwall systems contain aromatherapy units.

Both massage and aromatherapy sometimes use towels, and these will have to be cleaned by the laundry system.

### ■ Pet therapy

Pet therapy involves pet therapists bringing domestic animals (usually dogs) into the patients' rooms. If pet therapy is to be used, careful thought should be given to the choice of floor coverings. It might be the deciding factor to choose tile over carpet since animals may shed or soil the floors.

Alternatively a room can be allocated for pet therapy with a tiled floor and space for a wheelchair and a seat for the therapist.

### ■ Reflexology

Reflexology works on the principle that all nerve endings are on the foot and that careful massage of these reflex points can help relieve areas of stress in the body and relax the patient.

This therapy may take place in the patient's room, as it doesn't require specific equipment. This also requires towels and use of the laundry system.

Gentle music is sometimes used with complementary therapies and if so a music system will be required.

# HOSPICE DESIGN MANUAL

## Room Notes – Public Area

### RECEPTION

The reception area has the importance of creating the first impression.

Visitors (caregivers) may enter the hospice at any time day or night, and for security reasons it is important for the staff to know who is in the building at all times. For this reason all visitors should pass through a reception area. However, it's impractical to staff the reception counter continuously, so generally two separate entries are provided – one for daytime during regular office hours, and one for all other times.

During the former the reception would be located immediately after entering the building and will be manned either by volunteers or staff members. Here the visitor will be greeted, sign in (and out) and be directed where to go. A quiet room or area off the reception provides a place to break bad news to a visitor upon arrival.

A reception counter as such will be manned for eight or nine hours a day, and for the remaining 15 or 16 hours the on-duty nurses will be the only staff in the building (excepting cleaning and maintenance staff). During these times the doors will be locked.

It is therefore of high importance to provide the nurses with the ability to easily identify who is at the door and to safely let them in.

It is quite common for a relative to arrive from far away during the middle of the night and need to be let in to visit their loved one.

Either the nurses' station can be located close to the main entry to facilitate this, or there has to be a night entrance close to the nurses' area. In either case a closed-circuit TV system will allow the nursing staff to monitor the entrance during the night hours before having to open the door.

Quite often female nurses will be the only ones on duty at the hospice during the wee hours, and their security has to be taken very seriously. The entrance used at night should have no concealed area in which someone may hide. *(see Nurses' Station, Section 4, page 75)*

## Room Notes – Public Area (continued)

### SANCTUARY – also called Chapel, Meditation Room

A sanctuary in a hospice provides a space where one can come to terms with the recent death of a loved one or where anyone can seek sanctuary – patient, relative or staff member. It provides a quiet space for contemplation or prayer:

- It is possible to open it up to a larger area in order to be used for memorial services

- It should be non-denominational to accommodate those of differing faiths

- The design should encourage spirituality without relying on traditional religious symbolism

- Storage space for religious artifacts – crosses, stars, footbaths, etc., should be included

- Ideally the sanctuary will overlook a quiet garden and have direct access into it

- The use of stained glass is appropriate

- The sanctuary should be located near the bereavement suite if one is included

- It should be located near main entrance

- Multiple uses of the space may be considered such as music therapy

- It should not be located near any noisy area

In an area with a large Muslim population it may be possible to adjust the direction of the building so that the sanctuary faces Mecca. If not the direction to Mecca should be well marked.

## Room Notes – Public Area *(continued)*

### DINING ROOM

The requirements of the dining area closely follow the decisions made for the kitchen as to who will be provided with food.

In a large hospice where cooks prepare food for the entire facility it would call for a dining area of suitable size to accommodate everybody – especially if food is served for people using conference facilities who will all wish to eat at the same time.

If the kitchen provides food only for the patients and if their caregivers fix their own meals, then only a few tables will be needed. Dining areas provide a place for caregivers to sit down and chat to each other, and to be away from the patient area for a while.

The dining area can become an important social gathering place, but only if it is inviting – having it overlook an exterior space helps greatly.

Care should be taken where possible to give a nice scale to the dining area to keep it from looking like a canteen.

In a small hospice, the dining room may be set up as in a home with a large central dining table with overhead light. This can give a comforting homelike feel and ensure a canteen effect is avoided and as an extra benefit provide a space for staff or other group meetings.

Questions to be asked:

- Will patients eat in their rooms or be encouraged to eat in the dining room?

- Will nurses and other staff members prefer to eat in the staff break room – as a chance to get away for a while?

*(North Carolina regulations call for 20 square feet of dining space per patient. Other places have different requirements.)*

## LIBRARY

A hospice library can be anything from a complete library as part of the hospice's education center to a brochure rack in the reception area.

Information on palliative care, common patient conditions, and bereavement issues should be available to relatives and the general public to help them better understand the situations they face.

If a room is to be allotted for a library, it should have all the connections required for computer Internet access.

A library will most likely contain:

- reference works
- general hospice information
- reading materials for the relaxation of patients and family members

As such it will be used by staff members, the general public, and patients and their family members.

Because of the possible use by the general public it should be located close to the reception area.

## CONSULTING ROOMS

A variety of consulting rooms will be required depending upon the particular services offered by the hospice program.

They may be used by:

- Bereavement Counselors
- Social workers
- Physicians
- Chaplains
- Nurses

In many cases the consulting room may also be the worker's office.

Furniture arrangements will depend upon specific tastes of those using the rooms, but room should be provided for comfortable seating, desk space for the worker, and a wheelchair.

A room brightly lit with large windows makes the room less intimidating to those meeting with consulting staff.

# HOSPICE DESIGN MANUAL

## Room Notes – Public Area (continued)

### BODY REMOVAL / BEREAVEMENT SUITE

The death of a patient is usually handled in one of two different ways:

- Upon death, family members leave the room, the patient is cleaned up, and bed linen is changed. Family members then return and pay their last respects. The body is then removed directly from the room to the funeral home.

- Upon death, the patient is removed to a bereavement suite in the hospice and then to a funeral home, giving time for relatives to pay their last respects in the hospice setting rather than in a funeral home. British hospices usually include a bevereament suite.

In either case the deceased person should be moved as sensitively and discreetly as possible, not passing through any public spaces.

Certain religions call for the patient to remain in their bed for a certain amount of time to allow the soul to leave. Specific bedside rituals may also be called for and should be ascertained well before death.

Different state and local regulations specify the length of time a patient may remain in the room after death. These vary from state to state.

Rooms should have the ability to be cooled down with air-conditioning if a patient is allowed to remain in the room.

A bereavement suite would include a viewing room, and an adjoining private lounge area, with a bathroom. Ideally it would be connected to a private garden space. Facilities should be included for relatives to fix light refreshments.

It should be located so visiting relatives can access the suite directly from reception and not have a long walk all through the hospice.

The viewing room should be chilled, but not the lounge, which needs to be separately controlled.

Some hospices in Britain have temporary mortuaries to hold one or more bodies for a few days until a mortician can collect them, as some British funeral directors don't work during holidays.

A temporary mortuary can either be a refrigeratedroom to accommodate one or more gurneys or have slide-out type body drawers if more storage is needed.

## BATHROOMS

Adequate bathroom facilities will need to be provided throughout the hospice.

All bathrooms should be handicapped accessible, and all should be equipped with hand sanitizers.

Patient bathrooms should be also be fully assisted *(see Patient Bathrooms, Section 4, page 73)*

Excluding the ones for patients' the following bathrooms will be required:

- for visitors' use in patient area
- for nurses' and other staff in patient area
- for visitors' near reception
- for administrative staff in office area
- for conference/seminar participants (can expect high use at break times, requiring several rooms)
- for kitchen staff
- for day care patients
- for day care staff
- for family use in family suites

## SHOP

Hospices responsible for their own fund-raising often have a resale operation, with hospice stores throughout the community.

In addition, smaller items can be offered for sale in the hospice building. These usually includes such items as cards, mugs and trinkets etc.

Ideally a separate space should be provided for the shop, either a separate room or an alcove off the reception, as a display in the reception tends to look messy and can clutter up a reception area.

Some hospices also offer snacks and sandwiches for sale from the hospice shop.

If a hospice runs a resale operation, a large amount of storage space will be required along with office accommodations for the program manager. These do not have to be on-site.

# HOSPICE DESIGN MANUAL

## Room Notes – Service Area

### KITCHEN

Regulations differ from state to state as to equipment required in a hospice kitchen. Some states require a commercial kitchen if the hospice has more than 16 beds.

Local regulations differ too as to whether non-kitchen staff may enter the kitchen.

As a minimum, most states require a dishwasher capable of supplying water reaching 160°F minium to sterilize the dishes (such as the GE Profile series).

Care should be taken in planning for the future – to ensure there is enough space if a future addition will increase the number of beds and require a change from a domestic to a commercial kitchen.

A decision has to be made as to what food the kitchen will provide and for whom.

At one end of the scale the kitchen will provide three meals a day, seven days a week to the patients. At the other end, meals may also be served to the entire staff, conference participants, and family members.

Several options are available:

- A commercial kitchen with all the appropriate storage areas and equipment
- A smaller domestic-style kitchen operated by staff members

- A domestic kitchen in which relatives may come and cook meals as well as volunteers or staff cooking for patients
- A combination with designated areas for staff and for relatives, usually with separate appliances
- Two separate kitchens: commercial and small domestic

### Commercial Kitchen

The kitchen should be located adjacent to the service entry for food deliveries and for easy disposal of waste food and packaging waste into dumpsters.

Requirements:

- Dry food storage area, which should be unheated and windowless
- Freezer space, also in an unheated space
- Office area for cook/dietitian
- Dish- and pot-washing area separate from food prep/cooking area
- Storage for dishes
- Storage for food cart, and food cart loading/unloading area
- Changing area and bathroom for kitchen staff
- Double sink at least 42 inches wide
- Cleaning closet with mop sink

**KITCHEN** *(Continued)*

Because commercial refrigerators are very loud, a location just outside the food prep area yet close at hand is ideal.

Natural daylight and ventilation make the workplace much more tolerable for the full-time kitchen staff. Effective air-conditioning is important.

### Domestic Style Kitchen

A smaller kitchen along with the associated dining area may be treated more as in a home where the kitchen is the nerve center of the house.

The use of domestic style kitchen cabinets and appliances brings a different feel to a hospice and can help considerably in placing visiting relatives at ease.

Due to the smaller amounts of food and waste, the location next to the service entrance is not so critical. Food supplies are often brought in by volunteers shopping at the local supermarket.

As visitors enter the hospice, the smell of food cooking can be welcoming. However whilst the smell of bread baking or meals being prepared maybe attractive to healthy people, any smell can be nauseating to the very ill. For this reason the kitchen should not be placed in or right next to the patient area, and provision should be taken to ensure that patients can be separated from the smells.

A common practice is to have freshly baked cookies always available for family members, along with a pot of coffee. Quite often a separate refrigerator is provided for family members to place their own food in.

If it is decided to allow only staff in the kitchen by regulations or by choice, the domestic feel of the kitchen can still be achieved by use of a bar counter separating the kitchen from the dining area. Here family members may sit up at the bar and chat to the kitchen staff but be out of the way.

Requirements:

- Storage space for food cart, and food cart loading/unloading area
- Pantry with space for a freezer
- Adequate storage space for food and dishes
- Bathroom close by for kitchen workers
- Cleaning closet with mop sink
- Double sink at least 42 inches wide

## Room Notes – Service Area *(continued)*

**KITCHEN** *(Continued)*

Who will eat food prepared in the kitchen?

- Patients
- Caregivers?
- Extended families?
- Administrative staff?
- Nursing and medical staff?
- Day care patients?
- Conference participants?
- Volunteers?

Religious considerations:

'Kosher' for Jews and 'Halal' for Muslims are the terms used to describe which foods and drinks are acceptable for their consumption. Both religions have strict guidelines for food preparation especially with regard to meat. It is most important for Jewish and Muslim patients that these conditions are not violated.

Other religions also have dietary considerations and if the hospice service area has a high incidence of any ethnic groups, its dietary requirements should be studied, and understood by the kitchen staff.

Patients may also follow vegetarian or vegan diets which should be respected.

The kitchen should not be located too far from the patient area, avoiding a long trip back and forth through the hospice with a food trolley.

Doors encountered with the food trolley should be electrically operated.

## Room Notes – Service Area *(continued)*

### FLOWER ROOM

A flower room is commonly overlooked in hospice design.

Volunteers can rearrange flowers, donated by local funeral homes and from other sources, into smaller bouquets for distribution around the hospice.

Requirements:

- Separate entrance is desirable, but if not feasible the room should be located as close to the service entrance as possible.

- Windows that open, if possible, as the smell of many flowers can be overpowering in a small room.

- Should have utility sink and draining board, work area, space to store bouquets as they arrive and shelves for storing vases.

- Disposal area for unused and withered flowers and stems.

### USED LINEN ROOM

The used linen room is for the storage of dirty and soiled linens and bedclothes prior to either being picked up by a laundry service or taken to the hospice laundry.

Soiled laundry smells, so this room should be located well away from the patient or any public area.

The room should contain a utility sink to enable anyone handling dirty linens to immediately wash their hands.

The room requires negative air pressure and an air exhaust fan.

### CLEAN LINEN ROOM

The clean linen room is for the storage of fresh linens and should have an abundance of shelving and room to store the clean linen trolley.

## Room Notes – Service Area *(continued)*

### LAUNDRY FACILITIES

Laundry will be contracted or done in-house.

#### Contracted:

A laundry service will clean:

- Bed linens
- Nurses uniforms (if used)
- Kitchen uniforms
- Bath towels

Storage space for laundry carts next to the delivery entrance is needed.

A small patient area laundry room with washer and dryer will also be needed:

- Patients' pajamas and clothes
- Relatives' clothes
- Towels used for complementary therapy
- Hair salon towels
- Kitchen towels

The room should have space for an ironing board and adequate storage for cleaning supplies with bleach and any other chemicals in secure storage.

#### In-House:

This requires large commercial machines using high temperature water for infection control.

Areas required:

- Sorting
- Washing/drying
- Ironing
- Folding
- Storing

The laundry room requires good ventilation

A small patient area laundry room as previously described will also be required. This will generally be operated by hospice staff.

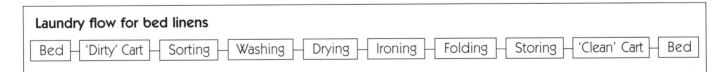

**Laundry flow for bed linens**

Bed — 'Dirty' Cart — Sorting — Washing — Drying — Ironing — Folding — Storing — 'Clean' Cart — Bed

## STORAGE

The most common complaint from existing hospices is lack of enough storage space.

Storage space is ideal to use up internal spaces.

Required Storage Spaces:

- Large Items: hoists, wheelchairs, mattresses, beds, comfy chairs, trolleys
- Nursing Supplies: dressings, gloves, etc. Should not be heated

    Medications require secure storage as per federal and state regulations
- Admin Supplies: paper, office supplies, computers, etc.
- Medical Records: As required by law. Becoming digital
- Linen: Clean

    Used (and room for cart)
- Cleaning: mop sink, trolley, vacuum, supplies. Secure storage for hazardous materials
- Kitchen: dry goods, fresh food, refrigerator(s), freezer(s) should not be heated
- Sanctuary: artifacts for all religions

- Flower Room: sink, vases
- Maintenance: lightbulbs, ladders, tools, etc.
- Physical Therapy: bars, exercise balls, cushions, canes, etc.
- Patient Rooms: patients' clothes and belongings
- Family Accommodations: clothes
- Coats: day care center, guests, visitors – in view of reception
- Living Room: childrens' toys, books, videos
- Garden: yard tools – mowers, trimmers, etc.
- Day Care Center: art supplies, large items – wheelchairs, hoists, chairs, etc.
- Classroom: folding chairs

Storage shelving should comply with OSHA regulations regarding height, depth of shelves, etc.

## Room Notes – Service Area *(continued)*

### CHANGING / LOCKER ROOMS

Those who work in the hospice and are required to wear a specific uniform need to be provided with suitable changing rooms.

Generally this would include nursing staff, kitchen staff, and occasionally physical and other therapists.

Requirements:
- Shower stall
- Lockers
- Bench

In a smaller facility one changing room will suffice with a lockable door (with a 'vacant/occupied' sign).

Larger facilities should have one for each sex.

A changing room with shower should be included even if uniforms are not required for any staff members.

Nurses are required to wear clean clothing. Should they get their clothing soiled, they need a place to clean up and change.

Adequate, secure coat storage should be provided for all staff members and near the main entrance for visitors.

### STAFF BREAK ROOM

A staff break room should be provided for nursing staff, volunteers, and other staff to get away from the patient area, to chat, relax, and prepare and eat meals and snacks.

It should contain a couple of comfy chairs or a couch, a dining table, and a kitchenette – counter with sink, small refrigerator, microwave, coffee machine, and cupboard space.

The room should be bright and cheerful. Direct access outside allows staff to step outside and smoke, but if so, it should be in a non-public space, not overlooked by patient rooms.

The break room should be located away from public areas to ensure that staff receive the privacy they need and are not overheard whilst chatting.

The staff bathrooms and changing rooms could be located adjacent to the break room.

## MECHANICAL / COMMUNICATIONS / ELECTRICAL ROOMS

The physical plant requirements will vary considerably from location to location primarily due to differences in climate. The requirements of a mechanical room will be directly related to the type of system to be installed and careful coordination will be required between architect and engineer.
*(see Mechanical Systems, Section 2, page 36)*

If the hospice will be hiring someone to oversee the physical plant and take care of building maintenance then space should be included in the mechanical room for a workbench and tool storage.

Care should be taken not to locate the mechanical room adjacent to a noise-sensitive area such as the sanctuary.

An emergency generator should be provided for back-up power in the event of power failure.
*(see Emergency Generator, Section 2, page 24)*

A communications room is a separate room used to house the telephone system, central computer, and interface for the computer ports in different rooms. It needs to be air conditioned.

An electrical room should be provided for the electrical panels in compliance with all applicable codes.

# HOSPICE DESIGN MANUAL

## Room Notes – Service Area *(continued)*

### CUSTODIAN'S ROOM and CLEANING CLOSETS

A custodian's room is required for the storage of cleaning supplies, and such items as toilet paper, soap, etc.

Hazardous cleaning materials should be stored in a lockable cabinet.

The room will usually require a mop sink, with mop storage, a utility sink, space for a cleaning trolley, space for a vacuum cleaner, and shelving/cabinets for the supplies.

The kitchen and laundry area may need separate, smaller cleaning closets each with a mop sink and appropriate storage.

Further cleaning closets may be necessary depending on the size and layout of the building.

### OXYGEN ROOM

If an 'oxygen farm' is to be used, a room or area should be provided to house a back-up system. This would consist of a manifold and oxygen tanks and would allow the delivery system to be switched over to a tank system should the oxygen farm fail thus providing an uninterrupted supply of oxygen.

The room requires internal and exterior access, ventilation, and must be fire rated as per local and state codes.

If a vacuum system is to be used, the vacuum pump ideally would be located in this room allowing all piping to run together. Care must be taken to avoid cross-connections between the two lines during installation. *(see Oxygen Supply, Section 2, page 37)*

## OFFICES

Office accommodation will be required for the following depending on the size and scope of the hospice program.

- Administrator / Manager
- Administrative assistants
- Secretary
- Medical director
- Nursing director
- Human relations manager
- Volunteer coordinator
- Fund-raising director and offices for fund-raising staff if necessary
- Physicians
- Therapists
- Counselors
- Chaplains
- Social workers
- Home hospice director
- Home hospice nurses

### General Office Notes

- Full-time office staff should be provided with natural light and ventilation.

- It is desirable to include the administrative staff within the hospice building to ensure a good connection and communications between the administration and medical staff, and avoid any alienation between the two.

- Office accommodation can be located on a second floor with elevator access.

- Open-plan offices should be avoided – due to the necessity of communicating with elderly people with hearing problems, several simultaneous phone conversations can be far too loud.

- Home hospice nurses require personal workstations to make phone calls and complete notes at the start and end of their day.

- The admin area requires appropriate bathroom facilities, and a snack/coffee area

- The admin area should be adjacent to the education classroom/conference room.

- The admin area needs a stationery store-room, a room for photocopying, and a mailing prep area.

- If fund-raising is a large part of the hospice program, a storage area near the office for paper goods should be provided along with large storage areas elsewhere for saleable goods.

- There should be direct access to the administration area from reception so that visitors to admin do not have to pass through the patient area, compromising the patients' privacy.

## Room Notes – Administration Area *(continued)*

### HOME HOSPICE DEPARTMENT

The majority of hospice care provided by most hospice groups in the U.S.A. is in the form of home care.

With home care, a team of nurses led by a home nurse manager and a scheduling coordinator provide hospice and palliative care to patients in their homes, with strong support from volunteers and family members.

Most patients have received home care before being admitted as in-patients.

Locating the home hospice department in the in-patient hospice building allows for easy communications between home nursing staff and the rest of the hospice team and allows home nurses to visit their former patients after being admitted as in-patients.

Home hospice nurses typically arrive in the morning, get their days' itinerary, make any phone calls, and head out to do the visits. At the day's end they return and complete the paperwork for the day's activities and make arrangements for the following day.

If the hospice has an on-site pharmacy, the home nurses can stop there to pick up the medications the patients require. Usually, though, they will stop at a local pharmacy and get them there.

Each nurse requires a soundproof workstation equipped with a desk, filing system, dictation machine, telephone, and computer connection.

Typically as many as 20 workstations will be required.

The department will also require a private office for the home hospice nurse manager and private office space for the scheduling coordinator, who meets with social workers, nurses and patients.

Office space will also be required for a medical record transcriptionist if this cannot be provided by the central administration.

## CLASSROOMS

Ongoing, on-site education for staff members and volunteers is an important component of any hospice program.

A flexible space is required which can be set up for round-table meetings or as classrooms with seating facing an audiovisual setup at the front.

In a larger facility a room divider would make the space more flexible.

An internal space is acceptable for ease of audiovisual viewing and minimizing distractions.

The room should have lighting which is suitable for a dimmer circuit.

They need easy access to a bathroom and should have at least a sink so that a coffeepot may be filled and cleaned (unless a snack area is close by).

## CONFERENCE ROOMS

Many hospices rent out space for other groups to use as a conference or seminar room. If this is done the conference room should be directly accessible from the main foyer and consideration given to hours of availability. If it is used during evening hours, will the rest of the hospice be open, or is it possible to isolate it from the rest of the building?

If conferences are planned, several bathrooms will be required to accommodate a rush of use at break time.

# Hospice Design Manual

## Room Notes

### DAY CARE CENTER

Day care centers provide a valuable service in giving ambulatory patients who live at home a place to socialize and to focus on various activities and diversional therapy whilst giving their caregivers a few hours respite. Typically a program will be for 15 patients, run from 10:00 a.m. until 1:00 p.m., and would usually include lunch.

The patients will be part of the hospice's home hospice program and generally one of a team of volunteers will pick the patient up and drop them off back home later.

An adjoining exam room allows a visiting physician to examine the patient if necessary, and other hospice spaces such as those for physical and complementary therapy, hair salon, specially equipped bathroom, and rooms for special procedures such as changing lymphedema dressings can be used by day care center patients

A day care center program makes patients comfortable with the hospice before they need to be admitted as in-patients when their sickness worsens. Day care patients may wish to visit friends in the in-patient unit.

#### Day Care Center Requirements:
- Sitting area
- Craft/activity area with sink
- Fully accessible toilet*
- Dining room*
- Exam room*
- Quiet interview room*
- Storage
- Office for day care center manager
- Snack prep area*

All must all be fully accessible

*Depending on the layout of the building and relationship to the rest of the hospice these areas may double up with areas provided for the rest of the hospice.*

#### Hospice Areas Used by Day Care Center Patients:
- Sanctuary
- Specially equipped bathroom
- Physical therapy room
- Complementary therapy room
- Hair Salon
- Special procedures

Direct access to a patio or courtyard is desirable. Participants may use the main hospice entrance or have a separate entry.

Consideration must be given as whether to allow patients to smoke and if so, where. If so, usually a covered exterior space is allotted, directly off the day care center space.

A designated smoking room could be doubled up with one for the hospice if such a room is provided. *(see Smoking Room, Section 4, page 78)*

If a day care center is not planned with the original building thought should be given to allow space for a future addition of a day care center as Phase 2.

# HOSPICE DESIGN MANUAL

## Section 5 – Schematic Designs

### Schematic Design Descriptions

### Scheme 1 Drawings

Ground Floor

Second Floor

Patient Room Plan

Addition A

Addition B

Day Care Center - Plan

Elevation – In-Patient Unit

Elevation with Day Care Center

### Scheme 2 Drawings

Floor Plan

Elevation

3-D View

# Hospice Design Manual

## Schematic Designs

To help illustrate the concepts outlined in this manual I have developed two schematic 'model hospice' designs.

These **do not** take into account the two most important factors with any design:

- Individual site constraints – views, direction of access, topography, aspect, etc.

- Individual requirements for a particular hospice – the scope of services to be offered, local differences, etc.

Both designs are planned for a fairly flat site with a pleasant southerly exposure and access from the west.

It must be remembered that for any design problems there are a multitude of solutions – as many solutions as there are designers. These designs are not meant to dictate a design for hospices, but merely to help illustrate the concepts outlined in this manual to help a hospice building function efficiently.

Scheme 1 is a large, full service hospice with 12 patient rooms (with a planned expansion to 24), a full range of associated services, on-site administration and home nursing services, conference facilities, and the ability to tie in with an adjacent day care center.

Scheme 2 on the other hand is a small eight bed facility which could be for a modest hospice program or a satellite facility for a larger program.

**Scheme 1**

Accommodations for the design:

- 12 patient rooms with the possibility of expanding to 24 in the future

- Four family suites

- Administration and home nursing services

- Conference/education center

- Day care center (planned so that it could be added as Phase 2)

- Full range of consulting/therapy services

- Commercial-style kitchen facilities to provide food for all of the above

- All appropriate auxiliary spaces

The basic goal and starting point of the design is to allow sunlight into each patient room at some point in the day, both initially with the 12 rooms and with an addition of a further 12 rooms. This places the rooms on the south side of the building, facing east, south and west.

The building, in order to accommodate all of the requirements, is large – approximately 37,000 square feet. To break down the mass, it is arranged around a large open courtyard, so as one progresses through the building, there are frequent visual connections into the courtyard, which allows daylight into all occupied rooms.

The courtyard also allows for outdoor dining in times of nice weather and provides a protected place for patients and family members to sit in the sun and for children to play. The patient rooms are arranged in two wings off the main building.

Body removal is designed to be as discreet as possible with a brightly lit corridor leading directly from the patient area to a covered transfer area.

A second floor with elevator access is utilized for the administrative staff, home nursing staff and suites for family members. The latter are located directly over the patient rooms, with a staircase descending into the patient area creating a homelike feel.

Exam rooms and special procedure rooms are located between the patient area and the public areas so that such facilities may be used by day patients as well as in-patients.

A conference/education center is located directly adjacent to the entry foyer so that participants do not have to wander all through the hospice.

Entering the building and turning left takes one to the public area; turning right takes one to the private, patient area.

A covered porch breaks the transition into the building and allows a place where someone may sit for a minute in a rocking chair and collect themselves before entering if necessary.

Externally a low roofline has been utilized to reduce the mass of the building, with all second-floor accommodation being provided with dormer windows. Different building widths create a variety of heights to further break up the mass and to create an inviting, non-institutional looking building which will reassure and feel comfortable to those entering.

This particular design would be built in the New England 'shingle style'.

### Scheme 1 – Detailed Room-by-Room Notes

### Patient Room

The patient rooms are arranged so that each one will receive direct sunlight at some time in the day, both in the original plan and with the planned additions.

Rooms face either west, southwest, south, southeast, or east and have direct access outside onto a private patio.

The entry into the room is recessed from the corridor, which serves the dual purpose of making the entry into the room less abrupt, and breaking up the corridor run. Double doors are shown with 1-foot and 3-foot panels. The 3-foot door is for normal day to day use but the smaller door may be opened to create a 4-foot opening to allow room to move beds, gurneys, etc.

The room layout ensures that the patient, from their bed, has a view outside, can watch television by

# HOSPICE DESIGN MANUAL

## Schematic Designs *(continued)*

looking straight ahead, and can see the room entrance to see who is entering or to look into the corridor if wanted.

There is space in the room for an easy chair next to the bed, and for a table and chairs or a couch for family gatherings. A table and chairs is preferred, as it provides an area for kids to sit up and play or draw, enabling them to be more relaxed during a visit than just sitting on a couch. It also allows family members to eat with the patient in the room.

The bathroom has a large sink vanity for personal items, and does not have a shower stall; rather the entire room is the shower stall, with a drain in the floor and a curtain on a track. This curtain covers the bathroom mirror when in use so the patient does not have to be reminded of their physical condition.

The toilet has drop-down grab bars allowing nursing staff access to both sides of a patient should the need arise.

### Nurses' Station / Medication Room

The nurses' station is located centrally between the two patient wings so that there is a line of sight along both corridors from a single, central position. The area backs onto the central courtyard, allowing daylight into the area and a door directly to the outside. Nurses can also monitor activity in the courtyard and access it quickly if their help is required.

Directly adjacent to the area is the night entry, enabling nurses to effectively control security.

There is also a view through the multi-use area to the southern garden area through French doors.

Adjacent, but separate from the main space, is the nurse manager's office, which has a private entrance, a door into the nurses station, and a window onto the courtyard.

The medication room is allocated in a similar position, directly off the nurses' station, also with a separate door so that trays or trolleys of meds do not have to pass through the nurses station. This room is also provided with a window, which makes it more pleasant, and faces onto the courtyard to alleviate security issues.

### Living Room

Located between the main entrance and the patient area, with room for children to play, with direct access onto a patio, and a cozy fireplace.

### Quiet Rooms

Initially two quiet rooms have been provided with two more planned into the subsequent additions. The first is located in the foyer and is where family members can meet with a nurse upon entry and be updated on the current situation. A second one is located in the patient area, would be equipped with a phone, and provides a cozy comfortable room for family members to 'get away' for a while, yet remain close at hand.

## Family Suites

The family suites are located on the second floor with elevator access and with stairs connecting to the central patient area.

With the initial design four suites are provided, located over one patient wing with the possibility of adding up to four more over the other wing. The accommodation is not luxurious but sufficient to be comfortable. Each suite comprises a bedroom and bathroom. The bedrooms have space for a double bed, sleeper sofa, and table and chairs.

Locating the suites on the floor above gives family members the comfortable feeling of 'going upstairs to bed' whilst still being close at hand and allowing them to have complete privacy and space to themselves 'away from the action'.

## Clean Utility Room

The clean utility room is located in the patient area directly next to the laundry delivery entrance.

## Dirty Utility Room

The dirty utility room is located in the patient area directly adjacent to the central area to minimize travel with bedpans.

## Used Linen Room

A room for used linens is located away from the patient area at the end of the service corridor adjacent to a covered exit.

## Clean Linen Room

The clean linen room is located centrally in the patient area.

## Specially Equipped Bathroom / Hair Salon

Located centrally in the patient area the room has a tub, shower, and a hairdressing area. There are windows on the outside wall, which would have opaque glass to enable the area to be bright yet retain privacy.

## Snack Bar / Computer Area

A multi-use area is provided in the central space between the two patient wings.

This would include a snack bar with tables and chairs, and a computer area with the monitors facing into the space enabling adults to supervise children using the computers.

The area opens directly onto the south-facing gardens through French doors.

## Therapy / Treatment / Exam / Consulting Rooms

All of these are located between the patient and public areas enabling them to be used by both in-patients and day care patients. They all face into the central courtyard to receive daylight and would be equipped with blinds to control privacy.

The physical therapy room has a high ceiling to allow a set of small stairs to be installed.

## Schematic Designs *(continued)*

The physicians have a combination office/exam room, but this could be separated into two smaller spaces if preferred.

Consulting rooms for services such as grief counseling are located directly off the main foyer.

### Reception

The reception is a room off to the side of the main entrance, with a window overlooking the entrance allowing the receptionist to monitor outdoor activity.

There is a small counter facing into the foyer to be as discrete as possible but providing a clear place where a new visitor to the hospice can check in.

### Sanctuary

Located in the public area the sanctuary is located along the building's main axis with direct access outside to a small walled garden, and across the corridor to the central court. Here the doors can be opened up to allow more space for a larger gathering such as a memorial service.

### Dining Room

A large dining room is included to allow seating for conference participants, all the staff, day care center patients, in-patients, and visitors.

Initially the dining room could be used as a small day care center prior to the construction of a separate facility.

Doors open off the dining room into the central courtyard allowing outdoor dining in fair weather, and onto a patio.

### Kitchen

A full commercial kitchen has been provided to cook for those eating in the dining room and for the patients eating in their rooms.

Located close to the service entrance the kitchen area has windows to the outside, an office also with windows, and several storerooms.

### Mechanical / Electrical / Flower / Oxygen / Sprinkler / Custodians' Room

These are all located in the service wing next to the service entrance.

### Staff Break Room

The staff break room is located between the service and patient areas, away from any public area.

It has an exterior door, allowing staff to step outdoors to smoke should they wish.

Attached to the room are the staff changing rooms, each with a shower.

Staff bathrooms are adjacent to the room.

## Administrative Offices / Home Hospice Department

These spaces are located on the second floor with elevator and stair access.

Office accommodation is arranged with several individual offices, two shared office spaces, and an open-plan home nursing office area for individual workstations. Also included is a snack area, bathrooms, storerooms, a photocopy/stationery room, and a classroom for in-house education seminars.

## Conference Room

A large conference room divisible into two smaller ones is located next to the main foyer with doors to a patio area and with two storerooms. It is close to public bathrooms and the dining room.

## Day Care Center

A day care center is planned as a subsequent addition, adjacent to the main hospice building, connected by a glass corridor.

The connection enables the day care center to take advantage of facilities in the main hospice building. A separate building enables the day care center to be built after completion of the main hospice building with minimum inconvenience.

The primary space in the main hospice building to be used by day care patients is the dining area, where lunch will be eaten most days. For this reason the day care center is connected into the dining area. Other areas used by day care patients will be the examination room, complementary therapy rooms, and sanctuary, located just beyond the dining area. Day care patients may also wish to visit in-patients and use the hair salon, which are just beyond the examination rooms.

The day care center itself has its own entrance and consists primarily of an open space with a cathedral ceiling, divided into three areas. The central space is a sitting room with space for up to 20 patients to relax and chat. This opens onto a patio/garden area and connects to the dining room of the main hospice building. On one side of the sitting area is a crafts area with a sink, counters, and a crafts table, and on the other side is a games area where patients may play cards and board games.

Also included in the building is a fully accessible bathroom, a mechanical room, storage, an office for the day care center manager, and a small staff area/kitchenette.

## Library / Shop

A small library/shop has been included directly off the main foyer.

## Schematic Designs (continued)

### Scheme 2

Accommodations for the design:

- Eight patient rooms
- Two family suites
- Domestic-style kitchen with adjoining dining room and living room
- One exam/consulting room
- Appropriate auxiliary spaces

In this much smaller design, all the patient rooms face in a southerly direction.

The main corridor is angled to reduce the impact of a long corridor.

As with Scheme 1, the entrance is through a covered porch to break the transition into the building and provide a place to sit.

The entrance leads into a domestic space containing a living room with fireplace, kitchen, and dining room. This 'public area' provides a reassuring homelike feel upon entering for patients and family members, and a comfortable space in which to 'hang out' during the visit or stay.

The patient area is directly off this 'living space', with a central nurses station and utility area. Also provided are two suites for family members, a specially equipped bathroom, hair salon, an examination/treatment room, and a screened porch.

A private quiet room is located between the patient and the public area.

Discreet body removal is through a door next to the screened porch.

Expansion is possible by extending either or both of the patient wings.

As with Scheme 1, this design is drawn in the New England 'shingle style'.

### Scheme 2 – Design Notes

Scheme 2 is arranged in two main zones – a public area upon entry, and a patient area beyond.

Entry into the hospice is through a front porch, which, as in Scheme 1, provides a place for someone to sit prior to entry and creates a transition between the outside and inside.

The front door leads into a living space with a living room, with fireplace, adjacent to the entry and kitchen and dining room straight ahead. The dining room opens onto a patio.

There is no formal reception, but there are two administrative offices adjacent to the foyer, one of which overlooks the entrance, enabling a staff member or volunteer to monitor the arrival area and greet visitors.

This 'living space' leads into the patient area, with a quiet room located in between.

Eight patient rooms are located in two wings, four rooms to a wing all facing southerly. One wing is angled to both visually break up the main corridor and create a slight sense of enclosure in the garden area in front of the patient rooms.

The route from the public 'living space' leads into a central sitting area between the wings. Off this area, central to both wings, is the nursing station and the service area, which contains pantry, storage, clean and dirty utility and linen rooms, with a covered loading area.

Patio doors lead from each patient room and the central sitting area to patios and gardens on the south side of the building.

The north side of the patient wing contains two family suites, the mechanical room, specially equipped bathroom, and a multi-purpose exam/consulting/therapy room.

A screened porch is located at the end of one wing. Body removal is through a door adjacent to this porch, out of view from the rest of the hospice and away from the service area.

## Scheme 1  Ground Floor Plan

1 - Covered Entry (2)
2 - Porch
3 - Foyer
4 - Reception
5 - Sitting Area
6 - Library
7 - Conference Room
8 - Sanctuary
9 - Dining Room
10 - Bathroom (6)
11 - Storage (4)
12 - Patio (5)
13 - Counseling Room (3)
14 - Complementary Therapy
15 - Living Room
16 - Kids' Nook
17 - Physical Therapy
18 - Nursing Office
19 - Nurses' Station
20 - Multi-Use Area
21 - Patient Room (12)
22 - Patient Bathroom (12)
23 - Quiet Room (2)
24 - Clean Utility
25 - Specially
     Equipped Bathroom
26 - Screened Porch (2)
27 - Night Entry
28 - Medication Room
29 - Doctor's Exam Room
30 - Pantry
31 - Dirty Utility
32 - Large Item Storage
33 - Dirty Linen
34 - Staff Break Room
35 - Staff Changing Room (2)
36 - Lymphedema Treatment
37 - Chaplain's Office
38 - Mechanical Room
39 - Electrical Room
40 - Sprinkler Room
41 - Oxygen Room
42 - Flower Room
43 - Maintenance
44 - Custodians' Room
45 - Food Storage (2)
46 - Kitchen
47 - Dieticians' Office
48 - Servery
49 - Elevator
50 - Link to Future Day Care Center
51 - Courtyard
52 - Gardens
53 - Funeral Director's Access

## Scheme 1  Second Floor Plan

1 - Manager's Office
2 - Assistant Manager's Office
3 - Volunteer Coordinator's Office
4 - Medical Director's Office
5 - General Office
6 - Home Hospice Nurses' Office
7 - Home Hospice Nurse Manager's Office
8 - Staff Break Room
9 - Classroom
10 - Storage (4)
11 - Photocopy Room
12 - Bathroom (3)
13 - Family Suite (4)
14 - Attic (Future Expansion)
15 - Elevator
16 - Courtyard
17 - Private
    Bathroom (4)

# HOSPICE DESIGN MANUAL
Scheme 1      Second Floor Plan

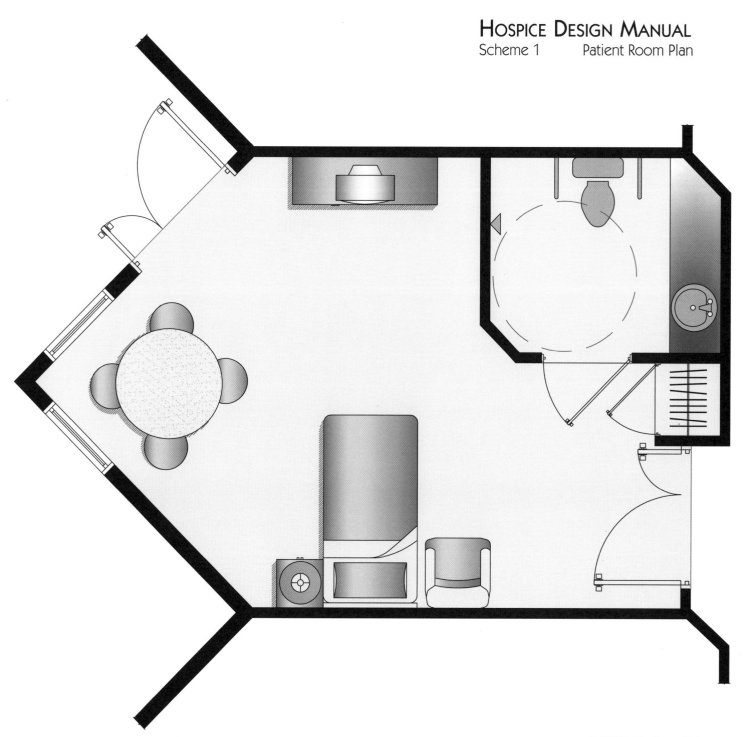

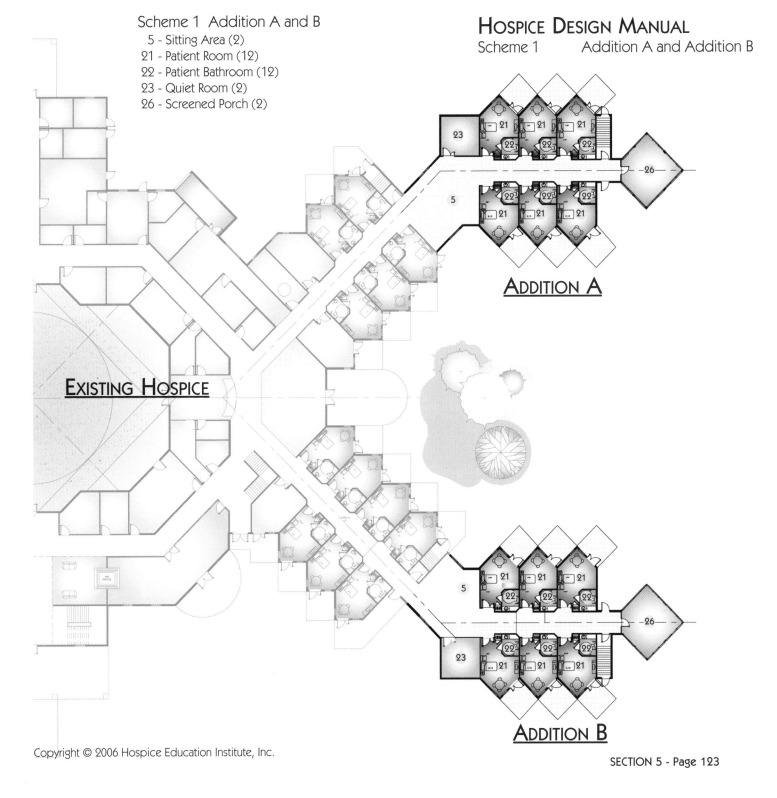

Scheme 1  Addition A and B
5 - Sitting Area (2)
21 - Patient Room (12)
22 - Patient Bathroom (12)
23 - Quiet Room (2)
26 - Screened Porch (2)

ADDITION A

EXISTING HOSPICE

ADDITION B

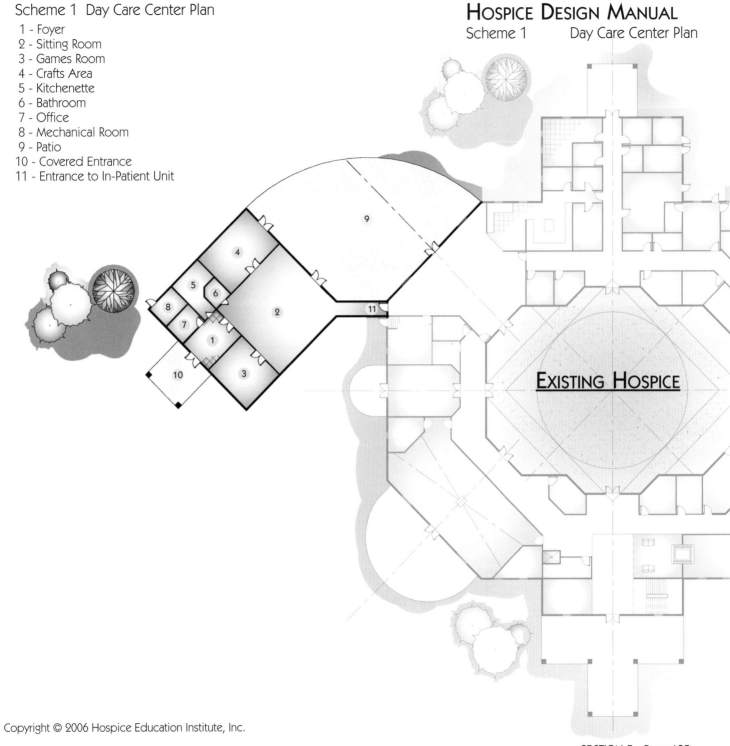

Scheme 1  Day Care Center Plan

1 - Foyer
2 - Sitting Room
3 - Games Room
4 - Crafts Area
5 - Kitchenette
6 - Bathroom
7 - Office
8 - Mechanical Room
9 - Patio
10 - Covered Entrance
11 - Entrance to In-Patient Unit

EXISTING HOSPICE

Scheme 1          Elevation with Day Care Center

## Scheme 2  Floor Plan

 1 - Main Entrance/Porch
 2 - Living Room
 3 - Dining Room
 4 - Kitchen
 5 - Office
 6 - Office/Reception
 7 - Quiet Room
 8 - Nurses' Station
 9 - Medication Room
10 - Familiy Suite (2)
11 - Patient Bedroom (8)
12 - Patient Bathroom (8)
13 - Specially Equipped Bathroom
14 - Exam/Consulting Room
15 - Mechanical Room
16 - Screened Porch
17 - Closet (2)
18 - Pantry
19 - Covered Service Entrance
20 - Corridor
21 - Dirty Linen/Utility

22 - Clean Linen
23 - Clean Utility
24 - Public Bathroom
25 - Staff Changing/Bathroom
26 - Nursing Supplies
27 - Large Item Storage
28 - Private Bathroom (2)

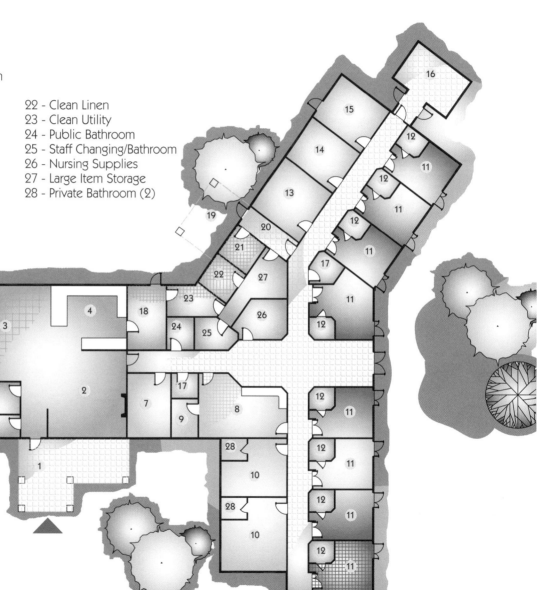

NORTH

## APPENDIX

Site Visits

Links to Suppliers

About The Author

## UNITED KINGDOM

- **Hospice in the Weald** – Tunbridge Wells
- **Keech Cottage Children's Hospice** – Luton
- **Macmillan Unit** – Christchurch
- **Mt. Edgcumbe Hospice** – St. Austell
- **Pasque Hospice** – Luton
- **Peace Hospice** – Watford
- **Pilgrims Hospice** – Ashford
- **St. Christopher's Hospice** – London
- **St. Clair's Hospice** – Hastingwood
- **St. Julia's Hospice** – Hayle
- **St. Luke's Hospice** – Winsford
- **St. Margaret's Hospice** – Taunton
- **St. Margaret's Hospice** – Yeovil
- **St. Michael's Hospice** – Basingstoke
- **St. Peter's Hospice** – Bristol
- **Treetops Children's Hospice** – Stoke on Trent
- **Weston Hospice** – Weston-Super-Mare
- **Wisdom Hospice** – Rochester

## UNITED STATES

- **Coming Home Hospice** – San Francisco, CA
- **Community Hospice House** – Merrimack, NH
- **Community Hospice of N. Central Florida** – Jacksonville, FL
- **East Pasco Hospice** – Dade City, FL
- **Four Seasons Hospice** – Hendersonville, NC

- **George Marks Childrens House** – San Leandro, CA
- **Good Shepherd Hospice of Mid-Florida** – Auburndale, FL
- **Hospice Home** – Elko, MN
- **Hospice House** – Monterey, CA
- **Hospice of Catawba County** – Hickory, NC
- **Hospice of Forsythe County** – Winston-Salem, NC
- **Hospice of N. Central Florida** – Gainesville, FL
- **Hospice of Richmond County** – Rockingham, NC
- **Hospice of Rutherford County** – Forest City, NC
- **Hospice of the Lakes** – Palatka, FL
- **Hospice of Union County** – Monroe, NC
- **Hospice of Volusia and Flagler** – Port Orange, FL
- **Hospice Touch** – Tomah, WI
- **Maitri** – San Francisco, CA
- **Nathan Adelson Hospice** – Buffalo St., Las Vegas, NV
- **Nathan Adelson Hospice** – Swenson St., Las Vegas, NV
- **N.C. Little Memorial Hospice** – Edina, MN
- **North Memorial Hospice** – Brooklyn Center, MN
- **Odyssey Hospice** – Las Vegas, NV
- **Pillars** – St. Paul, MN
- **Seasons Hospice** – Rochester, MN
- **Serenity House** – Santa Barbara, CA
- **West Pasco Hospice** – New Port Richey, FL
- **Wuesthoff-Brevard Hospice Care Center** – Viera, FL
- **Zen Hospice Project** – San Francisco, CA

## Links to Suppliers

Following are some links to various equipment and materials suppliers.
This list is by no means exclusive.

| | |
|---|---|
| **Arjo** | Bathing and patient handling systems<br>**www.arjo.com** |
| **Baxa** | Medical equipment including 'PhaSeal' – hazardous drug handling system<br>**www.baxa.com** |
| **Hill-Rom** | Headwall systems and accessories<br>**www.hill-rom.com** |
| **Invacare** | Bathing systems, furniture, and patient handling systems<br>**www.invacare-ccg.com** |
| **Marmoleum** | Flooring in which harmful microorganisms cannot live and breed<br>**www.forbo-flooring.com** |
| **Medical Products** | Full range of beds, furniture, wheelchairs, accessories, etc.<br>**www.medicalproductsdirect.com** |
| **Neaco** | Patient support systems, bath and shower doors, curtains and accessories<br>**www.neaco.com** |
| **Noram Solutions** | Bathing and patient handling systems<br>**www.norampatientcare.com** |
| **Penner** | Bathing and patient handling systems<br>**www.pennerpatientcare.com** |
| **Vancare Inc.** | Bathing and patient handling systems<br>**www.vancare.com** |
| **Volker** | Healthcare beds and furniture<br>**www.hertzsupply.com** |